SCHÖNING'S TRAVEL GUIDES

W9-AYB-065

THE BLACK FOREST

Text: Hans-Peter Wagner • **Concept:** S. Gödecke
Photo selection and design: S. Gödecke and R. Dohrmann
Fotos: Behrens, H. G. Bloem, F. Bormann, S. Cordes, Deike, Europapark Rust,
U. Findeisen, P. Finzer, S. Gödecke, Goerlipp Dia, Hansen/Drubba, R. Kandt,
H. W. Karger, W. Kraatz, F. Kübler, J. F. Lehmann, H. D. Linke, T. Marktanner,
R. Mayer, D. Minke, Neumann, W. Otto, E. Pflug, B. Radelt, C. Reinhard, W. Rost,
K. Rumpf, I. Sackermann, E. Spiegelhalter, H. Spiering, J. Suttner, D. Steffen,
W. Steiger, F. Thorbecke, R. Wittek, W. Wöhrle, Voutta
Cartography: Huber-Kartographie Munich
Edited by: R. Dohrmann Schöning-Verlag
Translated by: C. Watson

SCHÖNING
VERLAG

Overall production and © Copyright by
SCHÖNING GmbH & Co. KG
An der Hülshorst 5 · 23568 LÜBECK
Fon (04 51) 31 03-0 · Fax (04 51) 3 52 83
E-Mail: info@schoening-verlag.de
Internet: www.schoening-verlag.de
ISBN: 978-3-89917-142-6
8th edition

The Black Forest

The Black Forest – that brings to mind **pine forest** and **waterfalls**, **homestead with hip roof** and **cuckoo clock**, **bulb hat** and **Black Forest gateau**, **wanderlust** and **skiing holidays**. There's probably hardly any other **holiday landscape** with so many unmistakable features, though they give only an incomplete picture of the region. **Elegant spas** and **gourmet temples**, historic **churches** and **castles**, art and cultural artefacts and activities are other interesting aspects of the Black Forest.

But let's start with some sober statistics. The Black Forest stretches approx. **150 km** from **north to south** and on average **50 km** from west to east – and is thus the largest German holiday region. The borders are formed by Kraichgau in the north and the High Rhine in the south, the Upper Rhine in the west, and the Neckar and Baar in the east.

The history of the **Black Forest as a cultural region** began with what its name stands for: in a giant black forest.

The **Romans** called the impenetrable primeval forest covering the hills **"Silva Nigra"**. Like the **Celts** centuries previously, they shunned the inaccessible mountainous terrain and settled the Rhine plain and the valleys.

Then the **Alemannians** came in the third century AD. The wild tribes drove away the Romans and destroyed many of their fine settlements. However, they also established farmsteads, which later developed into villages. In the 6th and 7th c., the **Franks** assumed control and brought the Christian faith into the Black Forest. In their wake came **missionaries** from Ireland and Scotland. The God-fearing hermits also proved to be extremely intrepid.

There's a mill in the Black Forest valley ... even today mills are very much a feature of the Black Forest. Peacefully rippling water drives the mill wheels. The large number of sawmills in the Black Forest used to be driven by water.

They ventured into the primeval forest, where they built **monk cells** and small monasteries. The aristocratic lords had their sons educated by monks and also granted them land in impassable wooded areas.

The devout men gratefully accepted this challenge, and, thanks to their efforts, the entire Black Forest was gradually cleared from the 9th c. And it gained its name: in a document of St. Gallen Monastery the designation **"Saltus Svarzwald"** occurs for the first time in 868. The Black Forest people also have the monks to thank for the **"Sankt"** ("Saint") in quite a few place names. St. Blasien, St. Georgen, St. Märgen and St. Peter were named after the patron saint or the founder of the monastery in front of whose walls they were once established.

Mining in the Black Forest experienced its first heyday in the Middle Ages. Copper, lead, iron ores and silver were mined; **charcoal-burners**, shingle makers and coopers, who made the barrels, were the first craftsmen. Many aristocratic lords built fortified **castles** in the Black Forest from the 11th to 13th c. The **Zähringer**, a leading Swabian aristocratic family, was particularly active in this respect, founding for instance the towns **Freiburg**, **Offenburg** and **Villingen**. After the death of the last Zähringer, Duke Bertold V, the political situation changed in the land. The **Staufers** had to share their dominion with the Baden margraves and the counts of Urach-Fürstenberg. After the execution of the last of the Staufers, this era also ended in 1268. The **Habsburgs**, profiting from rivalries among the other sovereigns, then assumed power.

Many localities ruled by the aristocrats did not flourish in the 15th. and 16th c. There were also uprisings in the Black Forest, and the Reformation caused additional unrest. The **Thirty Years' War** (1618-48) brought much suffering in the towns on the main highways. During the War of the Austrian Succession a hundred years later, troops again passed through the Black Forest, torching towns and monasteries.

So substantial and agreeable – a Black Forest snack

Tradition and custom are still alive here, as the well-known bulb hat is worn on Sundays and public holidays and at weddings, as well as church anniversaries.

In 1803 **Baden** became an **electorate** and in 1806 a Grand Duchy. Württemberg became a **kingdom** in 1805. In 1818, Grand Duke Karl signed the Baden Constitution, which at that time was considered the most liberal in the whole of Europe. The two ruling houses shared the Black Forest and eased the lot of the farmers by abolishing the **tenth** and **compulsory labour**. They built schools, roads and the first railways. **Famine** struck in 1816-17, which forced many Black Forest people to leave their homes, but then prosperity returned.

Baden and Württemberg have formed the federal state **Baden-Württemberg** since 1952 following a referendum.

The Black Forest is the **highest German low mountain range**. With a height of 1,493 metres, the **Feldberg** towers over all the other **"one thousanders"** in the High and Southern Black Forest: Belchen (1,414m), Herzogenhorn (1,415m), Schauinsland (1,284m), Kandel (1,241m), Hochfirst (1,200m), Hochblauen (1,165m) and Hasenhorn (1,158m). Hornisgrinde (1,164m), Schliffkopf (1,055m) and Badener Höhe (1,002m) are the highest peaks on the Black Forest mountain road in the Northern Black Forest. Attractive **hills with views** in the Central Black Forest are Rohrhardsberg (1,152m), Brend (1,148m) and Brandenkopf (931m).

The Black Forest hills were created when the earth arched up about **sixty million** years ago along a tectonic weak point running south to north. At the highest point the crust collapsed, creating the present **Upper Rhine rift-valley** with the **Black Forest** on the right and **Vogesen** on the left. The spas of Bad Herrenalb in North Baden to Badenweiler in Markgräflerland have this **geological feature** to thank for their **warm thermal springs**.

In the last **Ice Age**, the **Feldberg** was the **centre of the glaciation** and was covered by a thick ice cap. In the **Hotzenwald** at the southern edge of the Black Forest, the masses of ice even met the Alpine glaciers. When the glaciers melted about **10,000 years** ago, they left behind numerous **cirque lakes** and **high moors**.

The **mild climate** in the forested low mountain locations of the Black Forest benefits many tourist communities, which are permitted to call themselves **"health resort"** or **"climatic health resort"**. However, there are considerable differences in temperature between the sun-drenched region around **Freiburg**, the warmest in the whole of Germany, and the high areas with their fresh winds.

The **Southern Black Forest Nature Park** – the role of which is to pre-

The trade in and above all production of the world-famous cuckoo clocks have developed into the main line of business in many localities in the Black Forest.

serve the unmistakable landscape and its habitats for flora and fauna – has existed since 1999. Its main areas are the **Feldberg area**, **Belchen** and **Wutach Gorge**, where more stringent nature protection provisions apply than in the other areas. The **Central/Northern Black Forest Nature Park**, whose catchment area extends from **Kinzig Valley** to the outskirts of Karlsruhe and **Pforzheim**, was founded almost two years later. There used to be nature reserves in the area of Kniebis and Alexanderschanze, on the Schliffkopf and at Wildsee.

The Black Forest is the **largest single forested area** in Germany. About two-thirds of its overall **area of 6,000 km2** is forested. The share of forest of the total area is somewhat higher in the Northern than in the Southern Black Forest.

The phenomenon of the **dying forest** is still a matter of concern. The acid rain, which brings the pollutants from the air into the ground, harms above all the coniferous trees: **fir**, **spruce** and **pine**.

The increasing **afforestation** of quite a few Black Forest valleys is also seen as a menace, as the balance between green meadows and dark forests not only constitutes the unique charm of the landscape, but also guarantees the highly praised **Black Forest climate**. The people of the Black Forest want to preserve both – for themselves and for all those who visit them to enjoy their hospitality.

The clock carrier is a well-known figure throughout the Black Forest, wandering from place to place carrying a large number of clocks on his back.
The "Uhrenträgerweg" ("Clock-Carrier Path") is a popular hiking route today.

Along the
Black Forest high road

The Black Forest high road, a **65 km** long section of federal highway 500, is the oldest German holiday route. It leads over the long ridge of the Northern Black Forest from **Baden-Baden to Freudenstadt**, providing access to the beauties and sights of an incomparable low mountainous landscape.

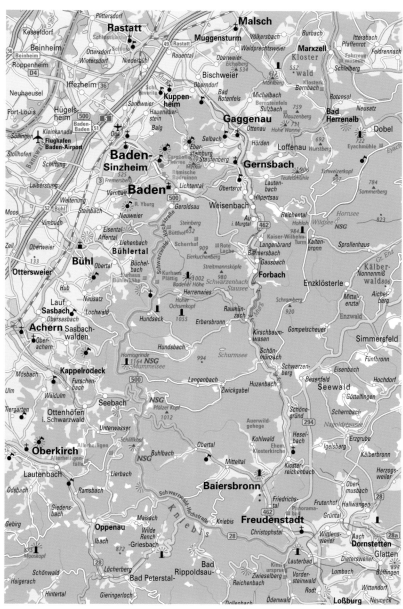

Baden-Baden
World-famous spa on the Oos

With its upper middle-class houses from the Gründerzeit (1871-3), elegant hotels and spacious parks, Baden-Baden, the **spa on the Oos (52,000 inh.)**, has retained something of the glamour of the Belle Époque right up to the present day. One also goes bathing here with style: in the magnificent **Friedrichsbad from the Kaiser's times** and the **Caracalla thermal baths opened in 1985**. The warm springwater was, incidentally, already enjoyed by the Romans in their settlement Aquae Aureliae in the 1st c. AD.

Baden-Baden's heyday began at the end of the 18th c. Its illustrious guests included **Bismarck**, **Queen** **Victoria** and **Czar Alexander**. The **spa centre** built by **Friedrich Weinbrenner** between 1821 and 1823 was already a focus of spa life at that time. And after the opening of the casino in **1838** in a wing of the spa centre, Baden-Baden became famous as the **"summer capital of Europe"**. The **pump room** with murals from the Baden world of saga is only a few steps away from the spa centre. Not far from the pump room, the three-tiered thermal fountain, a beautiful motif for photographers and a symbol of the town, bubbles away.

The **town centre**, which has been largely **free of traffic** since the building of the Michaelstunnel, offers various other sights. The **Catholic collegiate church** opposite the town hall was already mentioned as a parish church in **1245**. The tombstones of the margraves of Baden from the 14th-18th c. are on its choir walls. The **Russian church in Byzantine style** was built for the large

The first horse races in Iffezheim were in 1858. Here the elegant world met in the "summer capital of Europe".

View of the town

Russian community on Lichtentaler Strasse at the end of the 19th c.

The first performance in the **theatre on Goetheplatz**, a neo-baroque building, was given in 1862. The **market square** is dominated by the New Palace, a Renaissance palace, built in the mid-15th c.

on the remains of a castle. Baden-Baden's local hill is the **Mercury, 668 metres high** – the name derives from a votive stone for the Roman god Mercury. The top can be reached only on foot or with the **mountain railway**, which is 1,200 metres long. Visitors ascending the look-out tower are rewarded with a magnificent

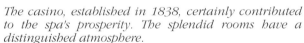

The casino, established in 1838, certainly contributed to the spa's prosperity. The splendid rooms have a distinguished atmosphere.

The pump room (above), built in 1842, and Festival Opera House, inaugurated in 1998 (l.)

cent panoramic view of the town and the gentle hill landscape in which it is embedded. The **Hohenbaden Castle ruins**, also called **Old Castle**, are on the western slope of the Battert. This castle was seat of the **margraves of Baden** between the 11th and 15th c.

That the name Baden-Baden still stands for glamour is guaranteed by the **Iffezheim race track**, where the celebrities meet at the annual international horse races. More glamour is provided by the **Festival Opera House**, which was inaugurat-

Theatre (l.) and Caracalla thermal baths (below), the name recalling its Roman origins

The famous Schlosshotel Bühlerhöhe, today frequented by political and business leaders

ed in 1998 and with its **2,500 seats** is the largest in Europe.

Above Baden-Baden, the Black Forest high road offers breath-taking views into the valleys and plain of the Rhine. This also benefits the high-altitude hotels such as the exclusive **Bühlerhöhe** and **Kurhaus Sand**. Quite a few beautiful lookout points are, however, a consequence of the storm of the century "Lothar", which swept over the Black Forest in 1999.

Kurhaus Sand

The Black Forest high road snaking over the hills

The lake, 290 metres long and 195 metres wide, is located in a deep basin at the foot of the Hornisgrinde.

Here the Lierbach, also called "Büttenstein waterfalls" and "All Saints waterfalls", plunges in several stages down to the valley.

Mummelsee

Many sagas are associated with the **Mummelsee**, idyllically located in a basin at the foot of the **Hornisgrinde**, **1,163 metres high** and thus the highest mountain in the Northern Black Forest. There are no fish in its marshy water, which is poor in oxygen, but mermaids and other water sprites are said to hide in it. The highest mountain lake of the Black Forest, located at a height of **1,030 metres**, was created as a **cirque lake** in a former glacial hollow. Measurements could not confirm the legend that the dark water is bottomless: the lake is 290 metres long, 195 metres wide and about 20 metres deep.

Mummelsee is one of the **most popular excursion destinations** on the Black Forest high road. Visitors can experience the fascination of the secret lake by taking a pleasant walk on the **path around the bank** or hiring a rowing or pedal boat.

Allerheiligen (All Saints), waterfalls and monastery ruin

The **All Saints Monastery ruin** is located in the wildly romantic Lierbach Valley between Oppenau and Ruhestein at a **height of 620 metres** below the Schliffkopf. Duchess Uta von Schauenburg founded the **Premonstratensian monastery** in 1196. For a time it was a **place of pilgrimage** and was given the status of **abbey** in **1657**.

Lightning destroyed the monastery church in 1804 – scarcely after the last monk had left the monastery after the secularization. The **collegiate church** – like the entire complex, built of coloured sandstone – was the first church built in Gothic style in Central Baden. Apart from parts of the nave and the porch, remains of the vestry and the **cloister** have been preserved. The ruins are still an impressive cultural monument today. An **information centre** has been set up in the former **servants' and farmworkers' quarters**.

The deserted ruins of All Saints Monastery, founded in 1196 by Uta von Schauenburg

The Büttenstein waterfalls below the monastery ruin were well known as **All Saints waterfalls**. Here the **Lierbach** plunges in several cascades **90 metres down** into the narrow valley. This tourist attraction was made accessible by paths and steps only in 1840. A **round foot-path** leads from the lower parking place over wooden bridges and steps through the gorge to the ruins of All Saints Monastery and then via **Engelskanzel** and **Rossgrund** back to the starting point.

Kniebis

This **pass at a height of 980 metres** near Freudenstadt is a popular starting point for hikes. It also used to have strategic significance, which is also recalled by the **Alexanderschanze**, built by Duke Alexander of Baden-Württemberg in 1734.

The Kniebis, one of the largest massifs in the Northern Black Forest

Freudenstadt

This **county town (23,500 inh.)** is one of the most important tourist spots in the Northern Black Forest. The **Kneipp spa due to the curative properties of its climate** – it gained this distinction in 1997 – is located on a plateau **728 metres** high. Freudenstadt, founded in **1599** by Duke Friedrich I of Württemberg, was destroyed in April 1945 and reconstructed retaining the **square streets of houses** according to the concept of the famous architect **Heinrich Schickhardt**.

A keynote of the town is the striking giant and almost square market place in the town centre. With its side lengths of ***216 x 219 metres***, this is the **largest market square in Germany**, a paradise for pedestrians and lined all around by **arcades**. The fountains are an important feature. The **town hall** with its tower and the town hall with the **museum of local**

The almost 5 ha market square forms the centre of Freudenstadt, marked off by arcades and lines of houses, built according to historic models. The town hall with its striking cupola is a noticeable feature in the northern part.

history and culture are interesting architecturally. Both were built after the second world war. An attractive building in the southern corner of the market square is the **Protestant town church**, a **right-angled building**, the congregation looking at the altar from two directions. The **Romanesque lectern** and the **baptismal font** from the 11th and 12th are exquisite features. The **modern spa centre** and the well-kept spa gardens are near the marketplace. An **historic visitor mine** recalls the days when miners mined heavy spar and silver. A good address for enthusiastic swimmers is the **panoramic bath** with several interior and exterior basins and a giant chute. There are also foot-paths and cross-country skiing courses.

The Protestant town church (1601), dominating the southern corner of the marketplace

The town hall with the museum of local history and culture in the centre of the square
The famous Bühl plums

Bühl and Bühlertal

The town of **Bühl (25,000 inh.)**, set in the middle of fruit plantations and vineyards, is widely known as the home of the famous **Bühl plum**, which is recalled by the annual plum festival in September. The health resort **Bühlertal (8,400 inh.)** with the wild **Gertelbach waterfalls** is located up to 1,000 metres above Bühl.

With its blossoming fruit trees in spring or grape harvest in autumn, the beautiful town of Bühl is very interesting to visit all year round.

Picturesque Bühlertal – here we see the district Obertal nestling harmoniously in the landscape.

15

Achern

The town hall square in Achern, meeting point for people of all ages

Achern (22,000 inh.) has the **Hornisgrinde** rising up 1,164 metres in the background to thank for its nickname "Hornisgrindestadt". Although it was mentioned for the first time in **1050**, Achern is very modern-looking: it was rebuilt after having been largely destroyed in the second world war. The oldest building is the **Gothic St. Nikolauskirche** from the early 13th c. A **scythe and local history and culture museum** presents the history of harvest equipment. There used to be a scythe works in Achern until 1965. The summer **steam train trips** on the **Acher Valley railway** between Achern and Ottenhöfen also awaken memories of times gone by.

Sasbachwalden

It's hardly surprising that with its magnificent half-timbered houses with their luxuriant flower decorations the centre of **Sasbachwalden**

(2,200 inh.), protected as a historic monument, is popular. The climatic health resort and Kneipp spa surrounded by vineyards can also claim to be the **most beautiful village in Germany**. The ruin of Hohenrode Castle, called **"Brigittenschloss"**, is worth seeing not only on account of the beautiful view – **Hohenrode** was one of the first stone fortresses in the Black Forest.

Kappelrodeck/Waldulm

Kappelrodeck and the district **Waldulm (5,850 inh.) are among the most well-known** German red wine communities and also a traditional fruit-growing area. In spring, **60,000 fruit trees** transform the valley into a sea of blossom.

The centre of Kappelrodeck is dominated by its symbol, the 11th c. **Rodeck Palace**, from where there is a splendid view of the Rhine valley as far as **Strasbourg**. The imposing **St. Nikolauskirche**, popularly dubbed **"Acher Valley Cathedral"**, is also worth seeing.

Impressive and majestic, Rodeck Palace thrones over the red wine village

Sasbachwalden, probably the most beautiful spot in the foothills in the Northern Black Forest

16

The water's crystal clear; a slight noise can be heard from the mill. Such an idyllic spot can be found on the "Ottenhöfen mill path".

Ottenhöfen

The health resort **Ottenhöfen (3,500 inh.)** is set in an attractive landscape, embedded in **ten side valleys** with hills, streams and numerous foot-paths. **Nine restored corn mills** and an intact **hammer mill**, which can be reached via a twelve km long round path offering many views, made Ottenhöfen a **mill village**. There are also about **200 schnapps distilleries** in the community area.

Interesting excursion destinations around Ottenhöfen are the pic-turesque **Edelfrauengrab waterfalls**, accessible via a **stepped path** with 180 steps, and the **Alpine-like Karlsruher Grat**.

Taking a trip through Acher Valley with the **steam locomotive "Badenia"** from the 19th c. is a special experience.

Ottenhöfen also gained literary fame: the American writer **Mark Twain** immortalized the place in his account of his travels in Europe.

Das Renchtal

The Rench has its origin in the Kniebis area at a height of 1,000 metres. In the upper part, the valley is narrow and steep like a gorge before opening out into a fertile plain at the main locality Oberkirch.

Renchen

The little town **Renchen (6,200 inh.)** also calls itself **"Grimmelshausenstadt"**. The baroque writer Johann Jacob Christoffel von Grimmelshausen (1621-76) spent some years here writing his most famous work, the novel **"Der abenteuerliche Simplicissimus"**. He is recalled by two monuments and the Simplicissimus house.

Main street of Renchen

Oberkirch

Vines, stone fruit and above all strawberries flourish in the mild climate at the exit of Rench Valley around **Oberkirch (19,500 inh.)**. The people of Oberkirch celebrate not only a wine but also a **strawberry festival**. The **ruin of Schauenburg Castle** is the symbol of the little town. The former fortress was built by the Zähringer Berthold II at the end of the 11th c. The famous poet Grimmelshausen was castle administrator

Ruin of Schauenburg Castle

18

between 1649 and 1660. The old town hall has a museum of local history and culture and Grimmelshausen museum.

Bad Peterstal

The well-known spas **Bad Peterstal** and **Griesbach** form a twin community (3,500 inh.). The curative properties of the **carbonated** springs were already well-known in the Middle Ages. The first large bathhouse was created in Bad Peterstal at the end of the 16th c.

The Rench quietly flows through the health resort Oppenau

Oppenau

Oppenau (5,500 inh.), a state-recognized health resort, was mentioned for the first time in the 11th c. After its destruction in a devastating fire in 1615, it was rebuilt according to the plans of the architect Heinrich Schickhardt. The **upper gate** has remained of the old town fortifications. The classicist **Catholic church** is worth seeing. The town hall has the **regional museum for the Rench Valley.**

View of Peter and Paul church

Bad Griesbach

Griesbach's upturn as spa also began in the 16th c. Even **Kaiser Wilhelm I** and **Czar Alexander II** visited it for a health cure. The place also acquired historic significance: in 1818 **Grand Duke Karl** signed the first **Baden constitution** here.

Bad Griesbach is known for its mineral springs, which were used long ago.

Das Murgtal

With its **80 km**, the **Murg** is the second longest river of the Black Forest. Its springs are at a height of 900 metres in the area of **Schliffkopf** and **Ruhestein**. In its upper part, the valley is sometimes as narrow as a ravine before opening out into a delightful landscape with fruit farms that was already settled in the High Middle Ages.

Rastatt

The county town **Rastatt (43,000 inh.)**, a traffic junction at the entrance to Murg Valley, was mentioned for the first time in **1084**. The **baroque palace**, used as a seat of a margrave in 1705, is regarded as the earliest and most exact imitation of Versailles. The palace has a military museum with exhibits from the Middle Ages to the present day as well as a freedom museum. The watertower (1900) at the edge of the town centre is the symbol of Rastatt.

The palace, focal point of Rastatt

The old town of Ettlingen, designed as a pedestrian zone

Ettlingen

The **baroque palace** in the centre of the old town of **Ettlingen (38,000 inh.)**, located at the end of the **Alb Valley**, forms the backdrop to an annual **palace festival** in summer. The town hall is also a baroque building. Ettlingen, which goes back to a **Roman settlement**, was mentioned for the first time in **788**. The **old fools' fountain** with the sculpture of the court jester Hansele von Singen is also worth seeing.

Gaggenau

The county town **Gaggenau (30,000 inh.)** is the **economic centre** of the Murg Valley, with **Daimler Benz AG** as the largest company. The locality was mentioned for the first time in 1288. The district **Bad Rotenfels** is known for the **Rotherma** modern **mineral thermal baths**. The first mineral spring was already discovered in 1839. There is a church with a 14th c. steeple in the district **Michelbach** and a **little baroque pilgrimage church** in the district **Moosbronn**.

Gaggenau

Gernsbach

The health resort **Gernsbach (15,000 inh.)** has had a town charter since

1248. **Rafting of timber** on the Murg used to be a source of wealth. The picturesque old town rises like a terrace on the left bank of the river. Interesting sights are the **Protestant Jakobskirche**, a 15th c. **church with naves of equal height** and the **Catholic St. Mary's church** (1378), which combines Gothic and modern elements. The **Storchenturm** is part of the old town fortifications.

Gernsbach, a romantic little town with half-timbered buildings on the left bank of the Lower Murg

Forbach mit Schwarzenbachtalsperre

The attractive Forbach (6,000 inh.) has been the location of a hydroelectric power station since 1928.

The symbol of the Murg Valley is in Forbach: the largest roofed-over and cantilever wooden bridge in Europe

The water of the **Schwarzenbach dam** is retained by a masonry dam 380 metres long and 65 metres high. **Surfing** is permitted on the **2.5 km long reservoir**. A popular photo motif is the **Forbach Murgbrücke** (1778), a roofed-over and self-supporting wooden bridge, the largest of its type in Europe. The district Bermersbach has the **Murg Valley village and local history and culture museum**.

The fjord-like appearance of the Schwarzenbach dam (1926) is apparent from the aerial photograph.

Schönmünzach

The health resort Schönmünzach, located at the junction of the Schönmünz with the Murg

The health resort **Schönmünzach** is an old glassmakers' and raftsmen's village. There are interesting destinations for hikers in its surrounding area, such as the idyllic **Wildsee** at the foot of the **Seekopf**, **1,055** metres high.

Klosterreichenbach

The Baiersbronn district **Kloster-reichenbach** in a very attractive location is known above all for its well-preserved **monastery church St. Georg** (1082). The abbot Wilhelm founded the monastery as priorate of Hirsau Monastery. The monks made an important contribution to the settlement of the region. The church with the two massive towers was built with local coloured sandstone and redesigned several times over the years. The **bath house** of the former **Benedictine monastery** is still preserved. The monastery gardens are today spa gardens. The small Protestant village church in Romanesque style in the district **Hesselbach** used to be a **forest chapel** of the monastery.

The past seems to have come alive here near the fine Reichenbach Monastery.

Baiersbronn with Obertal and Mitteltal

The **health resort Baiersbronn (16,000 inh.)** in the Upper Murg Valley with its 19,000 ha is the community with the largest area in Baden-Württemberg. Its core area, which dates back to the **13th c.**, forms along with **eight districts** a large community. The little **museum**, which is devoted to the

The well-known Hotel Traube-Tonbach offering top cuisine

Overview of Rosenplatz von Baiersbronn

story-teller **Wilhelm Hauff** (1802-27) is an original institution. The beauties of nature in the surrounding area include the wild romantic **Sankenbach falls**. The name Baiersbronn also stands for **top cuisine**. The districts **Mitteltal (Hotel Bareiss)** and **Tonbach (Hotel Traube)** are the best known among gourmets.

23

Pforzheim

The **"gold town" Pforzheim (116,000 inh.)**, world famous for its jewellery industry, is the starting point for long foot-paths and the **Black**

Pforzheim, gateway to the Northern Black Forest

Forest spa route. The town was mentioned for the first time in 1067. It was destroyed in February 1945 and today has modern functional architecture as well as some historic buildings that have been lovingly restored.

Dobel

The little spa and winter sports locality **Dobel (2,000 inh.)** above Bad Herrenalb and the romantic Eyachtal used to be a **woodcutters' and farmers' village** in the middle of the high fir forest. It has also been an attractive place for tourists since the 19th c.

Bad Herrenalb

The thermal springs make the friendly spa a popular health resort.

Bad Herrenalb (7,000 inh.) is a **climatic health resort** with a modern thermal movement bath. It has its origins in a **Cistercian**

monastery (1148). Visitor attractions are the **toy museum** with Biedermeier dolls and nostalgic steam train trips on the Albtalbahn.

Maulbronn

The picturesque **Maulbronn (6,300**

inh.) in Salzach Valley is known above all for its completely **preserved medieval monastery complex** (1147). The UNESCO included this in its list of **World Heritage** sites.

Bad Wildbad

Bad Wildbad (12,000 inh.), a

The little spa Bad Wildbad, regarded as the second "world spa" in the Northern Black Forest

popular spa in the valley of the Enz, has been the **state spa** of the state of Baden-Württemberg since 1824. It has the traditional Graf-Eberhard-Bad (PalaisThermal) and König-Karls-Bad as well as a modern thermal movement bath.

View of the beautiful health resort Enzklösterle

Enzklösterle

The health resort **Enzklösterle** owes its name to a small **convent** on the Enz, mentioned for the first time in **1145**. Its development has been closely connected with its heavily wooded surroundings. It has an **exhibition of cribs**, including the world's largest hand-carved crib.

Nagoldtal

The route through the approx. **45 km long Nagold Valley** is one of the most interesting in the Northern Black Forest with many notable historic attractions.

Bad Liebenzell

The spa **Bad Liebenzell (10,000 inh.)** features the **Paracelsus mineral thermal baths** and attractive spa gardens, as well as historic buildings such as the **parsonage** (1785), **old town hall** (1533) and the rebuilt **castle of the counts of Calw**.

The spa gardens in Schömberg, particularly attractive in the evening

Schömberg

The Kneipp spa **Schömberg (9,000 inh.)** is located in a sheltered high valley between Enz and Nagold above Bad Liebenzell. It is a popular place for holidays thanks to its beautiful location and unique opportunities for hiking.

The cosy little town of Bad Liebenzell, particularly the spa centre, is bathed in a warm light in the evening.

Hirsau Monastery

Hirsau **(2,000 inh.)** is a little place with a great past. The **largest German monastery** and the **largest Romanesque church** in Germany

Looking through to the Benedictine Hirsau Monastery

were built here on a plateau above the Nagold between 1082 and 1091. At that time, Hirsau was a stronghold of the papal party in the investiture struggle with the German king and a centre of the reform movement. This is recalled by the **monastery museum**. Open-air events are held in the monastery ruins in summer. Hirsau has also become well-known as a result of the poem **"Die Ulme zu Hirsau" by Ludwig Uhland**.

Calw

The **county town Calw (23,000 inh.)** in the central Nagold Valley used to be one of the richest towns in Württemberg. It was established from 1075 under the protection of the **castle of the counts of Calw**. The **old town centre** with its beautiful half-timbered buildings and the old town hall with a stepped gable is worth seeing.

Opposite the town hall is the house where the world-famous writer **Hermann Hesse** was born on July 2nd 1877 as son of a missionary and a missionary's daughter. Reflecting on his childhood, Hesse described Calw as **"the most beautiful town of all"**.

Calw, the former town of the salt and timber trade, is situated in the heart of Nagold Valley. With its well-kept half-timbered houses, it looks like something out of a picture book.

Hermann Hesse

The most well-known works of Hermann Hesse (1877-1962) are "Siddharta", "Steppenwolf" and "Narziss und Goldmund". His late work "Glasperlenspiel" is regarded as the highlight of his career.

Hesse won the Nobel Prize for Literature and the Goethe Prize in 1946 and the Peace Prize of the German Book Trade in 1955. In the 1970s and 1980s, he was the most-read European author of this century. He also had many devotees in the hippie scene, particularly as in his work he

Hermann Hesse

strove to harmonize western and eastern philosophy of life, the contrasts of the spirit and ethical being with nature and sensuous beauty.

The symbol of Calw is the **oldest stone bridge** over the Nagold with the medieval **Brückenkapelle** consecrated to St. Nikolaus. Since 2002, Calw has also had a sculpture of Hesse in honour of its most famous son, whose 125th birthday was celebrated with a comprehensive programme. The museum of the **International Hesse Centre** was enlarged on this occasion.

Hermann-Hesse-Platz.

Bad Teinach-Zavelstein

Bad Teinach-Zavelstein, known for its waters, set in the middle of Teinach Valley

Bad Teinach with its spa facilities is located below in the valley of Teinach and Nagold. About 170 metres above it is **Zavelstein**, a medieval **little castle town** protected as a historic monument with a ruin from the Staufer era. The **two localities** form together with five villages one community **(3,000 inh.)**. The **Teinach mineral springs** were already known in the Middle Ages. The Württemberg dukes had their summer seat here in the 17th/18th c. The **modern spa centre** was built in 1983 after a thermal spring was discovered during deep drilling operations.

Nagold

Nagold (22,000 inh.) is located at the juncture of the Black Forest and Gäu in a wide valley basin at the confluence of the **Nagold and Waldach**. Nagold's focal point is the historic **Schlossberg** with its impressive castle ruins and traces of settlement from Celtic times. The locality was officially **mentioned** for the first time in **786** as **"villa nagaltuna"**. The castle and town were razed during the Thirty Years' War.

The small old town with its **elliptical plan** has some fine half-timbered buildings. The town hall has a baroque facade. The old market square features a fountain sculpture of the **"wilde Urschel"**, a count's daughter from **Hohennagold Castle**, holding the Nagold town coat of arms in her hands. A symbol of the town is the **old tower** recalling the former **Marienkirche** from the 14th c.

The **Protestant Remigiuskirche** is located somewhat higher up on the cemetery site. It is even older than the town and was enlarged several times over the centuries.

The church's walls are decorated by paintings from the Gothic era. The

Nagold in its beautiful valley location

oldest residential building in the old town is the **medieval stone house,** which accommodates a **museum of local history and culture**.

The attractive fun baths in the bathing park are a modern feature.

Altensteig

The health resort **Altensteig (5,000 inh.)** is located on the ridge of a hill above the Nagold. Keynotes are the **Old Palace**, based on a medieval castle, and the **New Palace**, built in the late Middle Ages.

The round **"Historic Path"** leads past the most interesting buildings. These include a special house type of the North-Eastern Black Forest: the half-timbered house with wooden tiles or panelled with wood.

Altensteig is a member town of the "German half-timbered buildings route" leading from Neckar to the Black Forest.

Fountain in Turmstrasse in Nagold
View of the Old and New Palace of Altensteig

The many medieval half-timbered houses of Altensteig, seemingly interlocked, dominated by the town church

Pfalzgrafenweiler town hall

Spa gardens in Lützenhardt

Dornstetten

The **Barfusspark** in the district **Hallwangen** is the latest attraction of the little old town **Dornstetten (8,000 inh.)**. Sights in the town centre are the **market square** with beautiful half-timbered houses and fountains, as well as the **St. Martinskirche** from the 15th c. Dornstetten was mentioned for the first time in the 8th c. An historic silver mine can also be visited in Hallwangen.

Pfalzgrafenweiler

The rural spa and winter sports locality **Pfalzgrafenweiler (7,000 inh.)** is known for its mild climate. You can take pleasant walks along its network of foot-paths (140 km in all). Worthwhile destinations for excursions are the **nature reserve** with 200-year-old firs near Kälberbronn and the romantic **Zinbach Valley**.

Lützenhardt

The health resort **Lützenhardt (5,000 inh.)** belongs to the community Waldachtal. Sights are the Catholic **Herz-Jesu-Kirche** in neo-Romanesque style, the late baroque **Heiligenbronn pilgrimage church** above the locality and a saw mill from the 15th c. There is a **holiday village** on the outskirts of Lützenhardt.

Horb

The **town Horb (26,000 inh.)** is a traffic junction and industrial location on the Upper Neckar. Horb was mentioned for the first time in 1101. Some old buildings have remained in the **medieval town centre** above the Neckar. The limestone figure of

Marketplace of Horb

the Virgin Mary from the 15th c. in the former collegiate church **Heilig Kreuz** was known as **"Horber Madonna"**. The town hall (1765) is decorated by **facade murals**. The annual **Maximillian Tournament** in June recalling knightly days of old attracts many visitors.

Show of flowers on the market square of Dornstetten

The "No. 1" gateau
Black Forest cherry gateau

The **cherry gateau** vies with the **traditional bulb hats** as the symbol of the Black Forest. This delicious crowning glory of every festive coffee table has meanwhile conquered the entire world.

It goes without saying that **emigrants** also don't want to miss out the Black Forest cherry gateau even on the other side of the Atlantic. Though Black forest globe trotters were admittedly pretty astonished when they were also offered the speciality of their home region in far-off **India**!

The **Guinness Book of Records** recently inspired bakers from the Calw area to create the largest cherry gateau in the world with a **diameter of over 7 metres and weight of 4.8 tonnes**.

The cherry gateau consists of **three dark bottoms** filled with cream and **sour cherries**. There are various recipes for it, though one thing must never be lacking: the unmistakable **aroma** of genuine **Black Forest kirschwasser**.

Recipe

Ingredients for the bottoms: 100 g butter, 100 g sugar, 1 little packet vanilla sugar, 4 eggs, 70 g rubbed ground almonds, 100 g grated semi-bitter chocolate, 50 g flour, 50 g starch, 2 level teaspoons of baking powder.

Ingredients for the filling: 7 tablespoons kirschwasser, 0.5 l sweet cream, 750 g sour cherries from the glass, 1 tablespoon of crumbled or grated chocolate.

Instructions: Bake cake in a springform for about **30 minutes**, allow to cool and cut horizontally in **three parts**. Sprinkle the two lower bottoms with **kirschwasser**, cover with **cream** and fill with **cherries**. Cover the top plate and sides with cream and sprinkle with **chocolate**. Finally, apply cream rosettes on the gateau and decorate with **cherries**.

Kinzigtal

With its length of **95 km**, the **Kinzig**, which has its source south of Freudenstadt, is the longest and most fast flowing tributary of the Rhine from the Black Forest. Its valley has

Europe Bridge linking Kehl and Strasbourg

important transport arteries running from west to east. A **military and trading road** already led from Strasbourg to Rottweil in **Roman times**.

Looking over the Neptune Fountain to the Einhorn chemist's of Offenburg – showing how beautiful the capital of Ortenau is.

Tourism became important after the opening of the **Black Forest railway** in 1873.

Kehl

The **Europe Bridge** links **Kehl (33,500 inh.)** with the European metropolis **Strasbourg** in France. The Rhine no longer separates today: this is also demonstrated by the garden of the two banks, the joint project of the state horticultural show 2004, linked with a spectacular new pedestrian bridge.

Offenburg

The county town **Offenburg (58,000 inh.)** is the heart of the Ortenau, blessed with wine, sun and culture. The transport, economic and administrative centre of the Ortenau district regards itself as the **"Gateway to the Black Forest"**.

A Zähringer document mentions **"castrum Offinburc"** for the first time in 1148. The town seal with the open castle was first used in 1284. In 1689 troops of the French King Ludwig XIV set fire to the town, almost completely obliterating the late medieval townscape, only the **Capuchin monastery** (1641) remaining unscathed.

The people of Offenburg rebuilt their town all the more beautifully in the 17th and 18th c. The **baroque town hall** (1741), neighbouring Königshof (1806) and **Jewish ritual baths** (14th c.) are worth seeing. There are middle-class houses with magnificent facades and beautiful fountains in the pedestrian zone. The **Ölberg** (1524) near **Heiligkreuzkirche** is an art monument.

Offenburg played an important role during the **Baden Revolution**. In 1847 the "people's demands in Baden", the first democratic programme in Germany, were formulated in the inn Salmen.

Durbach

The **winegrowing community Durbach** enjoys an excellent reputation as home of the **Clevner (Traminer)** and **Klingelberger (Riesling)**. The Durbach Valley has 460 ha of vineyards. The wine village is dominated by **Staufenberg Castle**, a former knight's castle from the 11th c.

Gengenbach

The special charm of the little town of **Gengenbach (11,000 inh.)** derives from its intact **medieval atmosphere** with its fine half-tim-

Catholic church St. Heinrich in Durbach

Romantic Engelsgasse in Gengenbach

bered houses, parts of the town wall, towers and gates.

A **Benedictine abbey** was built here in the 8th c. The town was founded in the 12th c. and granted a town charter in 1230. The **monastery church St. Maria, a three-nave basilica** (1120) with a baroque tower, is today a parish church. Although the church has been changed with Gothic and baroque elements, its Romanesque structure has remained. The centre of the town is the market square with the classicist town hall and **market fountain with the stone knight**. The history of Gengenbach is related by the **fools' museum in the Niggelturm**, the **town museum in the Löwenberg house** with special exhibitions and the **timber rafting and transport museum** in the former gateman's lodge.

It's delightful to stroll through the old town protected as a historic monument with the Obertorturm, Löwenberg Palace and monastery church

Biberach

The holiday spot **Biberach (3,200 inh.)** has a beaver in its community coat of arms. The oldest document in which the community is mentioned as "Biberaha" dates from 1222. The **museum of local history and culture Kettererhaus** is one of the oldest buildings. Silver ore was mined in the 12th and 13th c. in the district **Prinzbach** located higher up. The ruin of the former **Hohengeroldseck** Castle from the 13th c. is located above the top of the pass between Biberach and Schutter Valley.

Zell am Harmersbach

The historic old town of **Zell a. H. (8,000 inh.)** has picturesque little lanes and nooks, remains of the former town fortifications, the **Hirschturm** and **Storchenturm** and half-timbered, and Jugendstil and classicist buildings. The **former free imperial town** was mentioned for the first time

Storchenturm in Zell a. H.

in 1139. It also became well-known as a result of the **Zell ceramics factory** ("Hahn und Henne" brand). Countless pilgrims visit Baden's most important **pilgrimage church Maria zu den Ketten** from the time of the crusades. Local history is presented by the Storchenturmmuseum and the well-known **Fürstenberger Hof in Unterharmersbach**, which is rural in character. The **Gröbernhof golf course** is in front of the gates of the town.

Oberharmersbach

Brandenkopf, 945 metres high, the local hill of the health resort **Oberharmersbach (2,600 inh.)**, is the **highest spot** in the Central Black Forest. A little museum in an old **warehouse (1761)** provides information on the history of the village, which was first officially mentioned in 1139. This includes a **mill** and an historic **oven**.

Zell am Harmersbach – main street and fools' fountain

Oberharmersbach – centre with town hall

Steinach

Steinach (3,900 inh.) has one of the most beautiful **baroque churches** (1750), the only one in Kinzig Valley with an **onion tower**. There is a **local history and culture and small distilleries museum** next to the symbol of Steinach, the half-timbered house Schwarzer Adler (1716).

Hausach

A new attraction in **Hausach (5,800 inh.)** is the digitally controlled model of the Black Forest railway, **Europe's largest model railway**. One of the oldest buildings in Kinzig Valley is the **Hausach "village church"** (1148), almost 100 years older than the town itself. The ruin of **Husen Castle** dominates the valley. The **Herrenhaus** (1760), accommodating a museum, is a striking building.

Wolfach

The **town hall** (1893) with its impressive sandstone facade and frescoes is a keynote of the extensive centre of **Wolfach (6,000 inh.)**. The town was mentioned as early as the 11th c. The **palace** (1681) with its **facade 100 metres long** is one of the largest in Central Baden. The traditional craft of **glass-blowing** is demonstrated for visitors in the **Dorotheenhütte**. The late Gothic **Laurentiuskirche** and the baroque **pilgrimage chapel St. Jakob** are worth seeing.

Oberwolfach

Mining once played an important role in **Oberwolfach (2,800 inh.)**, known since 1275. The mine **Grube**

Wenzel, one of the most important silver mines in the Central Black Forest, is now a very interesting visitor mine. The church **St.-Bartolomäus-Kirche** in the district Kirche is a jewel.

Haslach

The picturesque **old town centre of Haslach (6,900 inh.)** with its half-timbered houses is protected as a historic monument. This town, mentioned for the first time in 1240, has a long tradition as a **market and commercial centre**. The silver mine Segen Gottes in the district **Schnell-**

Wolfach town hall

Fools' fountain in Haslach
The district Oberwolfach

ingen is one of the most important historic mines in the Black Forest. The town's most well-known son is the priest and writer **Heinrich Han-** **sjakob** (1837-1916). Traditional Black Forest costume is exhibited in the former **Capuchin monastery**.

The little rafters' and tanners' town Schiltach, downriver from Kinzig

Schiltach

The health resort **Schiltach (4,100 inh.)** is a little town out of a picture book. The **historic old town**, mentioned for the first time in 13th c., features a unique half-timbered complex, rising **medieval market square with town fountain** and town hall from the 16th c. with its **merlon gable**. The town also has three museums. Old trades that are still practised include the last **leather tannery** of the Black Forest.

Traditional markets as well as the well-known **New Year's Eve procession** have been held in the town since the Middle Ages.

Schenkenzell

The symbol of **Schenkenzell (1,900 inh.)** is the ruin of a former **administrative castle** (1244), one of the oldest in Kinzig Valley. The former **Wittichen Convent**, founded as a retreat by the Beguine sister Luitgard in 1324, is located in the side valley of the Kleiner Kinzig. The **baroque pilgrimage church** features the tomb of the blessed. There is a **geological instruction path** in the vicinity.

Health resort Schenkenzell at Kinzig and Kl. Kinzig

The monastery church in Alpirsbach, which developed from a monastery settlement in 1095, is a very special architectural highlight.

Alpirsbach

The health resort **Alpirsbach (7,000 inh.)** in the Upper Kinzig Valley originated from the **Benedictine monastery** founded in 1095. It was later a monastery administration and training institution for priests. Only the gate tower of the first **monastery church** has remained. The **monastery complex** was altered several times over the centuries. The **vestry** from the 13th c. is one of the oldest Gothic structures in south Germany. The **late Gothic cloister**, where classic concerts that have gained a good reputation are regularly held in summer, is also worth seeing. An interesting contrast is provided by the late **Romanesque residential tower** on the site of the present modern **monastery brewery**. This belonged to a **moated castle** in the 13th c. The monks in Alpirsbach also cultivated the **art of glass-blowing**, which is demonstrated today for visitors.

The very informative museum for town history in the former monastery administration.

cirque lake, located at a height of 839 metres.

Loßburg

The health resort **Lossburg (6,500 inh.)** is located in a pass at a height of 665 metres in the Upper Kinzig Valley. Its name recalls its former aristocratic rulers. The **castle** was built between 1252 and 1272, and the locality was mentioned for the first time in 1282. The former castle hill is still identifiable near the **Protestant Jakobskirche** with a **tower from the Late Middle Ages**. The **Kinzig spring** and a recreational facility designed as **"Zauberland"** ("Land of Magic") is on the outskirts of the locality. The **drinking water dam Kleiner Kinzig**, which is accessible via foot-paths, is located in the surroundings of Lossburg.

An uplifting Lossburg spa concert

The pilgrimage church Mater Dolorosa from Kinzig Valley is well worth visiting

Bad Rippoldsau

The spa **Bad Rippoldsau**, which along with **Schapbach** forms a **twin community (2,300 inh.)**, is located at the foot of the Kniebis. Bathing guests here have appreciated the beneficial effect of the **highly carbonated springs** since the 12th c. The first **bath house** was built in 1490. Today **Bad Rippoldsau** has an **ultra-modern spa centre**. The **Klösterle**, a former priory with the pilgrimage church **Mater Dolorosa**, is on the way to the Kniebis.

The baroque church **St. Cyriakus** in **Schapbach** is also worth seeing. The first section of the **Hansjakobweg**, a 50 km long round foot-path, begins in the centre of the village. It is also worthwhile taking a trip to the idyllic **Glaswaldsee**, a round

Bulb hats and
Traditional costumes

Anyone seeing the **straw hat** with the soft **red bulbs** immediately thinks of the Black Forest, though strictly speaking this "trade mark" may be worn only by the women in **Gutach** and the neighbouring villages **Kirnbach and Reichenbach**. These three communities in the **Central Black Forest** are the home of the famous **traditional bulb hat**, which was created over 200 years ago. The red bulbs are, inciden-

tally, reserved for single women – after they wed, tradition dictates **black bulbs**.

The **Schäppel** can be seen throughout the Central and Southern Black Forest. It consists of colourful **glass beads**, **little silver plates**, **mirrors** and **glass balls**. The head-dress is small and dainty in **Hotzenwald**, large and expansive in **St. Georgen**. The broad-brimmed **straw hat** around which a ribbon is wrapped is typical for the **Elz Valley**. A high straw hat is part of women's traditional costume in the area **Villingen-Schwenningen**. It is tied under the chin with wide coloured silk ribbons.

Schäppele

cuckoo clocks
Black Forest specialities

Farmers' fare in the Black Forest used to be simple, being mainly what the farm produced itself. **Milk**, **butter** and **eggs** were supplied by the cows and poultry. A **pig** was slaughtered once or twice a year and sometimes also a calf or a chicken. The bread was baked from the farm's own grain in the **little bakery** next to the farmstead. Vegetables and potatoes came from the **farmer's garden**, fruit from the farm's own trees on the meadow.

Fresh ingredients and if possible **natural products** are still the strengths of the local cuisine to-day, and the famous **top restaurateurs** in the Black Forest also swear by these. However, here it's not just the much-praised **Baden cuisine** that determines what comes on the table. After all, the eastern edge of the region is undis-putedly **Swabian**, so in the Black Forest boiled **breast of ox with radish sauce** and **fried trout** is served as well as **pancake soup** and **ravioli**.

Traditional dishes are **Schäufele**, mildly smoked shoulder of pork, **Brägele**, fried potatoes with onions and bacon, and **Bibeliskäs**, a cottage cheese prepared with pot-herbs and eaten with fresh coarse brown bread or potatoes in their jackets.

A lavish farmer's meal is the **Schlachtplatte** with warm blood and liver sausage, grilled sausage, meat stew and sauerkraut. In addition to the classic bacon snack, Black Forest locals are also fond of a **salad with sausage** as a cold smack.

Gourmets are spoiled depending on the season with **fresh asparagus** with various types of ham and pancakes, exquisite **filled breast of veal** or tender **roast venison** served with forest mushrooms and spaetzle.

Black Forest snack

Fruit spirits

Black Forest cherry gateau

Gutach and Gutachtal

The narrow and steep **Gutach Valley** with the famous **Triberg waterfalls** and the **36 tunnels of the Black Forest railway** winds through the Triberg and Hornberg granite. The left and right sides of the valley rise up to 1,000 metres.

Then the valley gradually widens at the village Gutach and near Hausach sweeps into Kinzig Valley.

Gutach is well-known for its famous traditional bulb hats. The **traditional costumes and wedding processions** regularly attract large

Gutach Valley, a typical Black Forest landscape as if out of a picture book

crowds of visitors. A church was already mentioned in Gutach in 1275. The present **Protestant church** has a late Gothic choir, a beautiful **tabernacle** with **Secco paintings** and a **baptismal font** from that time.

The war **memorial** of a mourning woman in traditional costume by the sculptor and painter Prof. **Curt Liebich** (1868-1937) is a work of art.

Vogtsbauernhof open-air museum, Gutach

Lorenzhof ▼   *Schauinsland* ▲

The **Black Forest Vogtsbauernhof open-air museum** in Gutach shows the rural cultural history of the entire Black Forest on an area of five ha. Its **six fully furnished farmsteads uniting all functions under one roof** represent the typical building style of their region.

The **Vogt farm (1612)**, after which the museum was named, is the only building still at its original location. The **Hippenseppenhof** is the oldest museum farmstead, built in 1599 in **Furtwangen-Katzensteig** in the style of the Höhenhäuser. The **Schauinslandhaus** is the only building entered from the narrow side. A "Hotzenwaldhaus" with its deeply pulled down roof and the **Falkenhof** from Buchenbach-Wagensteig were also **rebuilt in original style**. A **day labourers' house**, built in Oberprech Valley in 1819, impressively conveys the cramped living conditions of the ordinary people.

Ancillary buildings for **sawing, milling, baking and distilling** can also be viewed. Historic food and useful plants are exhibited growing outdoors.

There is a **farmers' and medicinal plant garden**. But technology from long ago can also still be seen here – on the field or in the forge.

The museum really makes the past come alive.

Room in Vogtbauernhof

Hippenseppenhof

German clock route

The **German clock route**, opened in 1992, is the most recent tourist route in the Black Forest and is regarded as one of the **most attractive holiday routes** in Germany. The **320 km long** round route goes from **Villingen-Schwenningen** in **many loops** through the most beautiful **Black Forest valleys**.

Making clocks

Uhren-Weisser House of a Thousand Clocks, Triberg-Gremmelsbach

Hornberg musical clocks

Titisee-Neustadt, St. Märgen, Furt-wangen, Schramberg, Rottweil and Bad Dürrheim are some of the overall **30 localities** with museums and many sights related to the **Black Forest clock** along the route. Tradi-tional and technically sophisticated clock factories, **clock-making workshops** and ateliers of **clock-face painters** give visitors an idea of the craftsmen's work.

Rottweil

World's largest cuckoo clock in Schonach

Eble Clock Park Triberg-Schonachbach

47

Clock manufacture and its history

The **little bird** that opens the little door on the hour and tirelessly calls out **"cuckoo"** doesn't just hang in rustically designed Black Forest living rooms. The **cuckoo clock**, after all, is one of the most popular souvenirs. It's the most well-known **Black Forest clock**, but not the first. The first Black Forest timepieces, the clocks crafted toward the end of the **17th c.** in and around **Furtwangen**, resembled simple iron wall **clocks**. They were made of **wood** and had only an **hour hand**. The **ordinary farmers** built and sold them to improve their earnings.

There was already a real **clock-making industry** between **St. Georgen** in the north and **Neustadt** in the south in the 18th c. Many **farmers' sons** who could not inherit the family estate became **clock-makers**. Inventive monks in the **monasteries** made a major contribution to the **technical progress** achieved. **Clock-making** thus became a real industry in itself and was taken up by craftsmen such as **joiners** and **turners**, in addition to the farmers.

When people weren't satisfied any more with just figures on the clock faces, the **artists** came into play. In the 18th c. Black Forest clock painters created exquisite faces in baroque style – also for musical clocks and **astronomical** chronographs. The famous Bernau painter **Hans Thoma** (1839-1924) also earned his money painting clock faces in his youth.

Franz Ketterer from Schönwälder is regarded as the inventor of the cuckoo clock. The first documentary proof dates from **1762**. The **cuckoo** made its presence felt initially **only acoustically**. A little **bellows** drew the bird's note from a little whistle. The **little wooden bird** that appears in the gable of the clock and calls out is an invention of the **19th c**. The **decorations** of the cuckoo clocks were carved by hand, a new line of business for Black Forest farmers' sons.

Most sawmills used to be driven by water

Initially, fully **packed clock carriers** travelled the land and sold their merchandise. Later, **trading companies** were founded and Black Forest clocks went to the Netherlands, England, Italy, Spain, **Turkey** and **Russia**. There was even a large Black Forest **clock company** in the Near East.

In the **19th c.**, some family clock-making businesses were established that later developed into large companies, such as the world-famous **Junghans-Uhren**. The swift development of the industry was also promoted by the government of the day: the Grand Duchy of Baden **Clock-Making School** was founded in **Furtwangen** in **1850**.

49

Hornberg

Hornberg Palace

Hornberg musical clocks

The story of **"Hornberger Schiessen"** (a tale of much ado about nothing), which is played on the open-air stage, made **Hornberg (4,500 inh.)** well-known. It was founded at the foot of a castle around 1200. Hornberg has also a unique school: the **Black Forest mushroom exhibition for instructional purposes**.

Triberg waterfalls

The **Triberg waterfalls** is one of the most spectacular sights in the Black Forest. It's where the water of the Gutach plunges foaming and thundering down in seven steps over massive blocks of granite through a wooded gorge above the Triberg town centre. With its height of **163 metres**, the Triberg falls is **Germany's highest waterfalls**.

The **forces of nature** during the **thaw** and after **heavy rainfalls** are particularly impressive. The light rushing of water that can be heard from afar is a very typical sound in the little town of Triberg. A special spectacle is the magnificent **fireworks at the waterfalls** in late July, which makes the cascades shimmer in every colour imaginable.

The waterfalls is easily accessible via three **signposted routes**: the Naturweg, Kulturweg and **Kaskadenweg**. The natural show can be experienced close up from the Kaskadenweg. The **Kulturweg** leads to the Bergsee. Panels along the way provide information on flora and fauna and special features of the waterfalls area. Amiable regular

The Gutach falls foaming down to the valley. The Triberg waterfalls overcomes a height of 163 metres.

visitors at the falls are swarms of friendly **squirrels**. The **Dieterle's Schwarzwalddorf** at the entrance to the waterfalls is worth visiting.

View of Triberg town hall

Triberg

Triberg (5,400 inh.) became world-famous thanks to its waterfalls. However, the little town, located on the slopes of a **deep valley**, has much more to offer, such as the **Black Forest museum** with its large collection of **Black Forest clocks** and **barrel organs**, a model of the Black Forest railway and beautiful minerals. The **wooden carved room** in the **town hall** shows scenes of life in the Black Forest and gets visitors reflecting in a humorous way. The masterpiece (1926) is by **Karl Josef Furtwängler**, the **"Schnitzersepp"**.

The roots of the **Triberg pilgrimage** go back to 1644. The baroque pilgrimage church **Maria in der Tanne** with its beautiful high altar

Surrounded by dark forest, the pilgrimage church is really impressive.

View over the Bergsee

A visit to the Triberg Black Forest museum makes a memorable experience.

was completed in 1705. Next to the pilgrimage church is the **Mesnerhäuschen** in an attractive location. This small half-timbered house (1697) is the **second oldest building** in Triberg. The **village church** in the **district Nussbach** dates from the 17th c.

A popular excursion destination in the **surroundings of Triberg** is the **Stöcklewaldturm**. The **world's largest cuckoo clock** ticks in the **clock park** in Schonachbach below Triberg. The clockwork mechanism made out of limewood measures an impressive 4.50 x 4.50 metres. The pendulum weighs 100 kg.

Schonach

Schonach (4,400 inh.) is a popular venue for winter sports fans. Every year **international Nordic skiing championships** are held on the **Langenwald ski-jump hill**, 38 metres high, the home hill of the **Black Forest ski jumpers**. There is great rejoicing in the **skiing village** when local stars return home with **Olympic medals** and **world champion titles**. The **long-distance skiing route** to **Belchen** begins in Schonach. It is also the starting point of the **Black Forest skiing marathon** to Hinterzarten.

Schonachbach – the world's largest cuckoo clock

House of a Thousand Clocks

The clock in Schonach, for many years the world's largest cuckoo clock

Inside the world's largest cuckoo clock

Rohrhardsberg (1,163 metres) is Schonach's highest point. It is an approx. 1,300 ha protected area for plants and animals as well as a hiking and skiing area. A sight in the centre is the **baroque church** (1760), which was newly built between 1912 and 1914. The **parish Schonach** was founded by the barons of Althornberg around **1150**. The ruins of the first small church, said to have been built around 1100, are supposed to be under the

Schonach spa gardens, where you have time to rest and relax and feed the dear birds

present church tower. The **font** (1624) and **altar pictures** (1747/48) are among the oldest sacred objects. The **cuckoo clock** is also omnipresent in Schonach. In **1981** the **master clock-maker Josef Dold** set a record building what was **at that time the largest cuckoo clock in the world** in the form of a small Black Forest house. The clockwork mechanism is 3.60 metres wide, 3.10 metres high and 1 metre deep.

Looking towards the ski-jumping hill

Schönwald

The history of **Schönwald (2,500 inh.)** dates back to the **12th c.** At that time, the locality comprised some large farms, which cultivated the sunny high valley, protected from the wind. One of the oldest farmsteads in the Black Forest is **Reinertonishof in Schwarzenbach**, built in 1619.

Today Schönwald is an official **climatic health resort. Winter sport** has a long tradition at a high altitude of between 950 and 1,150 metres There are several ski lifts, about 200 km of tracked **cross-country skiing courses** and a **modern ski roller route**. Schönwald can call itself **home of the cuckoo clock**. The first model was designed by the inventor **Franz Ketterer** from Schönwald in **1730**.

The spa Schönwald, not far from Triberg

Summer and winter ski-jumping hill in Schönwald

Furtwangen

Clocks have played an important role in the history of **Furtwangen (9,800 inh.)**, which was the **centre of the German clock-making industry** in the 19th c. Today the town has the German clock museum with over **8,000 exhibits**. This collection, regarded as the most comprehensive of its kind worldwide, very impressively documents the history of chronometers. The idea for it was proposed in 1852 by the then director of the Grand Duchy of Baden Clock-Making School in Furtwangen, **Robert Gerwig** (1820-85). Gerwig is also the builder of the **Black Forest railway**. A special treasure is the **astronomical world clock** (1787). Worthwhile trips into the surroundings are to the local hill **Brend**, 1,150 metres high, with its high, with its lookout tower, the origin

View over Robert-Gerwig-Platz to the Catholic church

German clock museum in Furt-wangen

The Brend, one of the most beautiful hills with a view, from where you can look over large areas of the Central Black Forest when the visibility is good.

of the Breg, one of the two sources of the Danube, and the **Martinskapelle** from the 12th c., which is passed by many foot-paths and cross-country skiing courses. A typical **"heath house"** with **full hip roof**, the **oldest type of building** in the Black Forest, is the homestead of the small-scale farmers in the district of **Linach**.

Hexenlochmühle

With its **natural shingle facade** and two tirelessly clacking millwheels, the Hexenlochmühle near Furtwangen is a Black Forest farm as if out of a picture-book. It was built in 1825 and has been in family ownership since 1839 (now in the fourth generation). The **millwheels** are driven by water of the **Heubach**. The large **water-wheel** with a diameter of **four metres** and an output of 13 hp used to power an **upward-stroke**

and a **circular saw**.

Balzer Herrgott is a popular destination for hikers in the surroundings. An interesting sight is a **Christ figure of sandstone** that has grown so far into the trunk of an old beech that only the face is still visible. There are various **legends** concerning the history of the stone figure and how it came into the forest in the **headwater region** of the wild **Gutach**.

St. Märgen

The farming town of **St. Märgen (1,900 inh.)** is the home of the **"Black Forest Fox"** breed of horse. **Rosstag** is one of the largest festivals. St. Märgen is a **monastic settlement** from 1118. Its most striking building is the **pilgrimage church** with its **twin towers** rebuilt in 1907 after a major fire. St. Märgen is one of the birthplaces of the Black Forest clock,

Cows grazing idyllically in front of the St. Märgen monastery church, which has become a destination of many pilgrimages.

examples of which are to be found in the **monastery museum**. The **cross-country skiing centre** is an attraction for winter sports fans.

Interior of the Hexenlochmühle

The water also drives two mill wheels in winter, when this is possible.

The Hexenlochmühle, the quintessence of a Black Forest mill, is located deep in Kerb Valley. It is reached via winding paths.

57

Festively illuminated, the twin towers of the monastery church of St. Peter

St. Peter

St. Peter (2,400 inh.), located on the southern slope of the Kandel, is proud of its rich tradition. The attractive traditional costume with the richly coloured **Schäppel**, the magnificent head-dress for young girls, can be seen particularly at church festivals. St. Peter was also regarded as the typical Black Forest village by the producers of the postwar film **"Black Forest Girl"**, as they chose it as location in 1950.

The centre of the locality is the former **Benedictine abbey**, founded in 1093 by the Zähringer Duke Bertold II as **house monastery** and sepulchre. The monks had the Black Forest cleared, settled farmers, founded a **glassworks** and greatly supported clock-making. The **"father of clocks"**

Thaddäus Rinderle, in addition to making two globes that can be seen today in the library, also built a **world clock**, which strikes in the German clock museum in Furtwangen and demonstrates the inventor's mathematical expertise.

The **collegiate church St. Peter** and the adjacent monastery buildings burnt down four times in past centuries. The now **completely preserved 18th c. baroque complex** with its elegant **rococo library** is one of the most beautiful and most well-known buildings of its kind in southern Germany. It was designed by the highly talented Vorarlberg **architect Peter Thumb**. The monastery was closed in 1806.

The **church** with the two character-

in the evening

The interior of the monastery church seems to be baroque exuberance and gold wherever you look.

istic towers with **onion towers** is today the community's parish church. The interior is a **three-nave hall**. The altarpiece **"Maria Krönung"** (1661) is remarkable. The monastery buildings surround two idyllically located **inner courts**, where **concerts and dance performances in traditional costumes** are held in summer.

Numerous foot-paths and cross-country skiing courses intersect above the locality. There are also **Alpine downhill runs**. The **Lindenberg chapel** with an old **pilgrimage path** with stations of the cross is in the surroundings of St. Peter. A popular destination for excursions is the small **Plattensee**.

Traditional costume in St. Peter

59

Glottertal

The traditional costume of Glotter Valley presented in front of a shrine

The beautiful Glotter Valley is simply enchanting and corresponds exactly to what one imagines the Black Forest to be.

The elongated community **Glottertal (3,100 inh.)** was the most famous Black Forest village in the 1980s. The TV series **"Black Forest Clinic"** caused much commotion in the peaceful valley underneath the Kandel. Everyone wanted to see the hospital in which the **TV Professor Brinkmann**, played by Klaus Wussow, operated. In reality, it is a **rehabilitation centre**. Many visitors and buses stop in front of its gates even today. The building was built in 1894 and recalls the time when Glotter Valley had a **sanatorium**. The first reference to the former **Glotterbad** dates from 1488. The locality was mentioned for the first time in 1112.

Vines flourish on steep southern slopes at the entrance to the Glotter Valley. This **highest vineyards** in Germany are supposed to be here. Quite another picture is offered in the lower part of the valley with its imposing Black Forest farmsteads. There an old corn mill, **Hilzinger Mühle** (1621), can be viewed. For **nature lovers** it is worth taking an excursion into the beautiful **Föhren Valley**, a side valley of the Glotter.

A short look back to the silhouette of St. Peter

Kandel

The **Kandel**, **1,243 metres** high, dominates the Black Forest hills between **Elz Valley**, **Simonswälder Valley** and **Glotter Valley**. In the Middle Ages, it was regarded as the Black Forest **"Blocksberg"**, haunted by witches and demons. There are two **round foot-paths** on the summit. The Kandel is also a **sporting paradise for hang-gliding fans**.

Waldkirch

Waldkirch (20,000 inh.) is the centre for the construction of **mechanical musical instruments**. The first **barrel and fair organs** were built here 200 years ago. The town stages an **international organ festival** every three years. The **Elz Valley museum** has an interesting collection of **nostalgic musical instruments** as well as **traditional costumes** from the Elz Valley and exhibits illustrating middle-class and rural home life.

The Kandel, 1,243 metres high, the local hill of Waldkirch

The town of Waldkirch, which has been able to preserve much of its original charm, in the centre of Elz Valley

61

Elztal and Simons-wäldertal

The six communities in the Elz Valley and the neighbouring Simonswälder Valley present themselves as **"two valley land"**. The two valleys form a **splendid holiday landscape** with height differences of up to 1,000 metres. When the fruit trees bloom in the **wine locality Buchholz** at the entrance to the Elz Valley, the hills are frequently still covered with snow. **Hörnleberg**, 907 metres high, a well-known **place of pilgrimage for the cult of the Virgin Mary** with a long tradition, is located between the two valleys. A **"Capellam uf dem Hörn-lin"** was already mentioned in **1469**.

The Elz Valley museum of Waldkirch in the former provostry building

Waldkirch, which was awarded the **federal prize for tourism and the environment**, goes back to a convent founded in 918. The former collegiate and now parish church **St. Margaretha** is a **baroque building** that is worth seeing. The **ruin of Kastelburg**, built above the town in the 13th c., gives an impression of medieval castle architecture. The **Black Forest Zoo Waldkirch** has brown bears, rock goats, sika deer, nandus, kangaroos and emus, a wild game reserve where animals can be stroked and a play arena.

Elzach

A **carnival figure**, the **Schuttig**, made **Elzach (7,000 inh.)** famous. The figure of a fool with fire-red shaggy garb, snail hat with woollen bulbs and terrifying wooden mask dominates the town from Shrove Sunday to Ash Wednesday. The processions with up to **1,200 Schuttig** figures put Elzach in **a festive festival mood**. The **health resort** in the Upper Elz Valley was mentioned for the first time in 1290. Sights in the town centre include the chemist's and the inn Löwe from the 16th and 17th c., as well as the choir of the parish church St. Nikolaus (1522).

Beautiful Elzach in the romantic Elz Valley. It's a worthwhile destination on the German clock route.

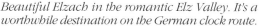

Schuttig fountain

Young Black Forest girls in the beautiful traditional costumes of the Oberprech Valley

The 19 km long **Hirtenweg** in the district **Yach** has richly illustrated **info panels**, informing the hiker, for instance, why the farmer runs behind the cow.

The health resort **Oberprechtal** above Elzach offers unspoilt nature, old farms, beautiful customs and well-kept foot-paths.

Simonswald

The houses and homesteads of the **five localities** forming the community **Simonswald (3,100 inh.)** since 1974 are distributed through the entire valley. The **Jockenhof village museum** in an old farm in **Obersimonswald** gives an impression of traditional rustic life. This historic building dates from around 1640. The **mills of the valley** – Kronen-Mühle, Schwanen-Mühle, Wehrlehofmühle and Oelmühle – can be reached via a **round path** beginning in **Simonswald**. The **Zweribach waterfalls** near Obersimonswald is also a popular destination for hikers.

Simonswälder Valley still has some farmsteads and hamlets.

The market fountain of the five-valley town Schramberg, a meeting place for old and young

The town garden and Lorenzkirche of the holiday town St. Georgen create a comforting and relaxing atmosphere.

The Albert Schweitzer house shows much about the chosen home of the "jungle doctor" Albert Schweitzer.

Schramberg

The name **Schramberg (18,700 inh.)** stands for the **clock industry** and **"Da-Bach-na-Fahrt"** of the fools, a jolly spectacle on Shrove Monday. Schramberg was founded as market centre in 1547, about 90 years after the building of **Hohenschramberg Castle**. Sights are **St. Maria**, one of the most important late classicist **churches** in south Germany. The **town hall** is adorned with an **astronomical clock**.

Tennenbronn

In **Tennenbronn (3,800 inh.)** a **Black Forest clock carrier** in traditional costume still appears – at the evening entertainment laid on for tourists. The **health resort** at the **Upper Schiltach** has its roots in the 12th c. A curiosity ended only in the 20th c. with the uniting of the communities of **Protestant** and **Catholic Tennenbronn** that had been separated according to confession.

St. Georgen

St. Georgen (13,800 inh.), located between 800 and 1,000 metres above sea level, is where original **nature** and **high technology** meet. The place has its origin in the **Benedictine monastery** founded in 1084. It received the **right to hold markets** in 1507 and was granted a **town charter** in 1891. The construction of the **Black Forest railway** (1873) speeded up its development, as related by the **phonograph** and **clock museum** in the town hall. The **Klosterweiher open-air swimming pool** is used as an ice rink in winter.

Königsfeld

An unusual man is honorary citizen of **Königsfeld (6,100 inh.)**: **Albert Schweitzer**, who received the award in 1949. The **Albert Schweitzer house** was inaugurated in summer 2001. This house where the Schweitzer family used to live has an exhibition on the life and activities of

Albert Schweitzer

Albert Schweitzer (1875-1965) *got to know Königsfeld in* **summer 1911** *because of the illness of his then bride Helene, who as* **nurse** *was recovering from tuberculosis in the spa. When Albert Schweitzer returned to Lambarene in Gabun in West Africa to work in his jungle hospital in 1923, his wife and daughter moved into a house of their own in Königsfeld. The climate did Helene Schweitzer good. The Schweitzers remained until 1933, her* **daughter Rhena** *attending the* **Zinzendorf Grammar School** *and also boarding school for a time. Helene returned to her house in 1947. Albert Schweitzer stayed regularly in Königsfeld when he was in Europe. In addition to his humanitarian work as doctor, Albert Schweitzer was also a* **theologian, philosopher** *and* **organist**. *He played and practised on the* **Königsfeld organ** *for his concert tours in Europe. He wrote parts of his book* **"The Mysticism of Paul the Apostle"** *in his Black Forest home.*

Waldau Castle ruins, one of the most popular destinations for excursions around Königsfeld

famous jungle doctor. Königsfeld was founded by the **Bohemian Brethren**, who settled in the Black Forest at the beginning of the 19th c. The building with the impressive **church hall**, built in 1810 as spiritual focus of the Protestant community, is in the centre of the locality.

Remains of the only **moated castle** from the Stauffer era in the further surroundings are to be seen in the district of **Burgberg**. The former lords of the castle were mentioned for the first time in 1116. The **Waldau Castle ruins** in the district **Buchenberg**, the keep of which has remained preserved, also date from this time.

Doniswald, also called **Eichhörnchenwald**, belonged as farmers' wood to the nearby **Donishof**. It became the first **spa gardens** of Königsfeld 160 years ago.

▼ *Centre of the Bohemian Brethren*

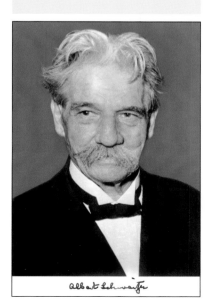

65

THE FOOLS HAVE IT THEIR WAY

In contrast to the exuberant merriment of the Rhine carnival, the **Swabian-Alemannian carnival street celebrations**, called **"Fasent"** or **"Fasnet"** depending on the region, also have a serious side, which recalls the origin of the custom.

In the carnival strongholds of the Black Forest, the high time of the buffoonery begins early in the morning on Dirty Thursday, **"Schmotziger Dunschtig"**, when people are woken up by "cater-wauling". **"Schmotzig"** comes from "Schmotz", which is Alemannian for fat or dripping, recalling that on this day the Fasnetsküchle delicacies are prepared in floating fat. On **"Schmotziger Dunschtig"**, the kids are let off kindergarten and school. The mayor is relieved of his office and has to hand over a symbolic town hall key to the fools. The Fasnacht is proclaimed or rung out at many places during the morning.

Leaping fools or parades of the local fools' guild with guest guilds as well as local associations and bands can be seen between Shrove Saturday and Tuesday.

The most well-known fools' court convenes in **Stockach** on Lake Constance. The **"Grobgünstige Fools' Court"** prosecutes top politicians. In **Tiengen** local VIPs have to justify themselves before the **"Criminal Court"**.

A declining custom is the **"Schnurren"**, **"Strählen"**, **"Hecheln"** or **"Aufsagen"**, at which fools, protected by a mask and disguising their voice depending on the custom, can tell the people on the street or in the inn what they think or make unfavourable comments on various follies and misfortunes.

The variety of the **Swabian-Alemannian** carnival figures is impressive particularly in the street parades. The **oldest** figures, already documented in the **late Middle Ages**, are the devil and the **wild man**, mostly a type of sylvan. With their guild of witches, the people of **Offenburg** awakened the **witch figure** to new life. All carnival celebra-

ALEMANNIAN CARNIVAL

tions in the south-west feature **"Fleckle"**, **"Blätzle"** or **"Spättle"**, one of the oldest disguises. The **"Häs"** is mostly linen garments on to which round or diamond-shaped patches of cloth are sewn.

The **"Hansel"**, **"Hansele"** or **"Narro"** is very common on the **Baar** and in the **Black Forest**. He is known as **"Weissnarr"** in the **Rottweil** and **Villingen** carnival. His garb or **"Kleidle"** is a white, two-part linen suit.

The mask, called **"Larve"**, is of wood and painted. The "Weissnarr" also has the **"Gschell"**, belts of bells carried on the chest and crossed over the back.

Hansele

In **Donaueschingen**, the **"Hansele"** is accompanied by the unmasked **"Gretle"** in traditional costume. "Hansel" or "Narro" are called such different figures as the **Furtwangen** **"Spättlehanseli"**, the **Wolfach** **"Nussschalenhansel"** and the **"Bändelenarro"** from **Zell am Harmersbach**. The joker or court jester figures like the **Wolfach** **"Schellenhansel"** are rarer.

The swarms of **"Hemdglonker"** ("Glonker" is Alemannian for "idler") in their white nightshirts with faces often made-up white who go through the roads and lanes making a racket on "Dirty Thursday" are not organized in fools' guilds.

Rottweil leaping fools

"Nussschalenhansel", an essential figure in the Alemannian carnival

The spire of the Kapellenkirche, 70 metres high, reaches majestically up into the sky of Rottweil.

Rottweil

Rottweil (25,700 inh.), the **oldest town** in Baden-Württemberg, is located on the border between the **Black Forest** and **Schwäbischer Alb**. The history of the former **imperial town on the Neckar** goes back to the time of the makers of band ceramics **(2000 BC)**. Findings from the time of the **Romans**, who left clear traces, are shown in the Dominican museum. The **"Rotuvilla" royal court**, mentioned for the first time in 771 AD, obtained great significance as court and administrative centre under the Carolingians.

The colourful, richly decorated oriels of the so typical middle-class houses in the main street of the oldest town in Baden-Württemberg

The **Rottweil manorial court** was one of the most important courts of the German kingdom in the Late Middle Ages.

The people of Rotweil have the **Staufers** to thank for their present **town centre**. They planned the town in the **Late Middle Ages in Zähringer style**, dividing it up with a main street crossing. The **town museum** shows a model of Rotweil in the Middle Ages. The **middle-class houses with their oriels** and the numerous **churches** date from this time.

In the 16th c. Gothic **Heiligkreuz-münster**, the **Apostle Altar**, **Altar cross** and "**Rottweiler Madonna**" are particularly impressive features. The spire of the **Kapellenkirche** (1340), 70 metres high, with its decorative figures is regarded as a cultural monument. However, the most well-known building in Rottweil is the **Schwarzes Tor** (Black Gate), through which the fools leap during carnival. The **Neckarburg**, sited high above the Neckar valley outside the town, is worth visiting.

The Black Gate of Rottweil is not really black.

Strong, reliable dogs have made the name Rottweil world-famous. As **herd dogs**, they used to keep the herds together in the former **Rottweil cattle trading centre**. The **Rottweiler breed** has officially existed since 1907.

Rottweil leaping fools

The carnival customs in Rottweil are among the oldest and most traditional in the area of the Swabian-Alemannian carnival.

The Rottweil carnival begins on January 6th, Twelfth night.

Then the "Abstauber" go through the town to free the Rottweil fools' clothes and hand-carved masks of limewood, the "Larven", from dust.

The "Franzenkleidle" (l.) and the main figure of the Rottweil carnival, the "Federahannes" (r.)

The main carnival days begin with "Schmotziger Donnerstag", the Thursday before Fasnetsmontag (Shrove Monday), on which numerous groups go through the town and into the pubs and restaurants. The groups make ironical comments on the events of the past year, mostly misfortunes and goings-on in the town.

The morning of Shrove Sunday is the time of the proclamation, at which the government of the town is transferred from the mayor to the fools' master. The fools' guild then rules until Ash Wednesday.

The "Geschell" has a lot to carry: the 48 small bells weigh about 13 kg.

The "Schantle", the nice old gentleman who was once a wild lad

The mask of the "Biss" is to be distinguished from the other masks by the mouth, which looks like an "8" on its side.

70

The "Bennerrössle" are the attraction during the leaping of the Rottweil fools. Two drivers try to keep the Rössle on track by snapping and whipping.

The **guild of fools** now rules until Ash Wednesday. The **parade on Sunday afternoon** is for the children and young people, associations and groups.

The **highlight** is rung out on **Shrove Monday** from the **Black Gate**. Punctually at eight, when the first bell rings, there's commotion behind the historic gate. The famous **leaping of the Rottweil fools** is introduced by horsemen bearing the standard of the imperial town. To the music of the **"Old Hunter's March"**, the "Narrensamen" with the **"Long Man"** stream into the wide upper main street, followed by the **"Narrenengel"** ("Fool's Angel").

He is followed by the various figures of fools to the sounds of the Rottweil fools' march: the **"Schantle"** with elegant umbrella, walking at a slow, leisurely pace and the "Gschellnarren" in white motley with a "Biss", which makes them look grim. The "Federahannes" in plumed cape, who dares bold leaps with his long pole, is always making fun. The **"Fransenkleid"** dances to the rhythm of the fools' march, the little bells on robe jingling. Things get wild with the advent of the **"Bennerrössle"**, whipped by their drivers down the main street. The **"Guller"** also marches along, sometimes almost going under amid all the buffoonery.

The "Federahannes" personifying the devil, one of the oldest carnival figures

71

Trossingen

Trossingen (15,000 inh.), located at the edge of the Black Forest, is home to music. In **1827 Christian Messner** brought the first **mouth organ** to the town, which has existed since 1797. The **German harmonica museum** in Trossingen also exhibits accordions, harmoniums and Jew's harps. The museum of local history and culture **Auberlehaus** exhibits **skeletons of dinosaurs** found in Trossingen and also operates the **oldest electric railway** in standard gauge as museum railway.

Bad Dürrheim

February 15th 1822 is a memorable date in the history of **Bad Dürrheim**

Spa centre

Narrenschopf

Colourful flowers decorate the paths in

(12,600 inh.), as on this day a **salt dome** of "excellent quality" was developed at a **depth of 345 ft**. This marked the start of the growth of the old **unplanned village** in the eastern **Baar**, which was mentioned for the first time in 889 as **"Durroheim"** in a document of St. Gallen Monastery.

The two wooden towers are salt spring shaft houses.

...he spa gardens leading to the fountain

The salt water, 28° warm, was used for bathing from 1851. The Baden Grand Duchess Luise had a **children's saltwater bath** built in 1883. Dürrheim was given the title **"Bad"** ("Spa") in 1921, **"Heilklimatischer Kurort"** ("Climatic Health Resort") in 1976 and **"Sole-Heilbad" ("Spa with Salt-Water Therapeutic Bat**hs") in 1985. The modern salt-water baths and Solemar health centre, a magnificent bathing area under glass and in the open air was opened two years later. Very recently, Bad Dürrheim obtained two further titles: **Natural Forest Community and Solar Community**.

Salt water and mineral bathing centre Solemar – the focus is on

The spacious spa gardens **"Luisengarten"**, named after the meritorious Grand Duchess, with its precious old trees, formed the centre of the state horticultural show in 1994. A **rose and natural remedies garden**, a round water basin and a natural pond were created and art objects installed.

The park also has the **Narrenschopf**. The museum of the Swabian-Alemannian guilds of fools has **about 400 fools' figures** with mask and garb. Other sights are the **Salinenpark** and **museum of local history and culture**.

73

Aerial photograph of Villingen showing how its centre is framed by the old town wall

Pedestrian zone Obere Strasse

Münster Unserer lieben Frau, the centre of the town

The founding of the twin town **Villingen-Schwenningen (82,000 inh.)** at the border between the **Black Forest and Baar** in 1972 was the largest project of the Baden-Württemberg administrative reform. At that time, nine outlying communities were added to the two towns.

The **Baden Villingen** and **Württemberg Schwenningen** have interesting town stories that can be traced far back in history. Villingen was mentioned in writing for the first time in a document of Emperor Ludwig the Pious on **June 4th 817**. In 999 Emperor Otto III granted it the **right to hold markets**, **mint coins and impose customs duties**. After almost five hundred years of affiliation to the House of Habsburg as former Anterior Austrian town, Villingen became a town in the **Grand Duchy of Baden** in the 19th c. At the same time, it underwent industrialization, which produced well-known companies in the 20th c.

Schwenningen was also mentioned for the first time in the 9th c. The locality passed to the **House of Württemberg** in 1444. At the end of the

20th c. it already had a **considerable industrial sector** focusing on **clock manufacture**. In 1907, the village, at that time the **largest** in the **Kingdom of Württemberg**, was granted a **town charter**.

Villingen still has the remains of the **town fortifications** from the 13th c.: the **Riettor**, Bickentor, Oberes, **Kaiserturm**, Romäusturm and **Pulvertürmle**. It is a perfect example of the characteristic street layout of the **Zähringer towns**. The old town is today a pedestrian zone plastered with stone mosaics.

The centre is formed by the **Liebfrauenmünster**, which was built in 1130 and altered several times over the centuries. The old and the new town hall are at the **Münsterplatz**. The old town hall, mentioned for the first time in 1306, has a fine late Gothic **stepped gable**.

The former **monastery complex** of the **Capuchins** (1268) is also part of the old town. The former **church with naves of equal height** is today a **concert hall**. The **Franciscan museum** has some interesting folkloristic and handicraft collections.

The focus of the town centre of Schwenningen is Muslenplatz with its **historic** and modern elements. The oldest buildings are two half-timbered houses from the 18th c. The history of Schwenningen is presented by the **local history and culture and clock museum** in the old teacher's house and clock industry museum in a clock factory. At **Schwenningen Flugplatz** there is an aviation museum, the showpiece of which is a Russian **"Antonov 2"**, considered to be the largest biplane in the world.

Both districts have well-kept park areas – Villingen the **Kneipp healthcure area in Brigachtal**, Schwenningen the Mauthe-Park, named after a clock factory owner. The historic Neckar spring is in the Schwenningen town park.

Muslenplatz, Schwenningen's focal point

Clock industry museum of the industrial town

Historic Neckar spring

"Brigach and Breg bring the Danube"

Flowing into the Danube

"Brigach and Breg bring the **Danube**," the Black Forest people say. The second longest river in Europe has its origin here. The **Danube** covers **2,800 km** up to where it flows into the Black Sea. The **Brigach** has its source at a height of **925 metres** at St. Georgen, the **Breg** at a height of 1,078 metres near **Furt-wangen**. They unite in **Donau-eschingen** and form the source of the Danube. The Breg spring is only about 100 metres away from the **Rhine-Danube watershed**.

Donaueschingen

Donaueschingen (21,500 inh.) has the Danube not only in its name: in the **palace park** of the **Fürsten-berg residence** there is a circular basin with a sculpture which was declared to be the **source of the Danube** in the 18th c. For the people of Donaueschingen, the **Donaubach**, which meets with Brigach and Breg at the edge of the town, is the actual source of the Danube.

The famous source of the Danube, surrounded by a grating, in the palace park

The prince's palace is a delight for the eye not only from the outside – inside there are also real treasures for those interested in history.

Donaueschingen is undisputedly an old town: it was already mentioned for the first time in a **royal document** in **889**. It achieved special significance in **1723**, when Prince Josef Wilhelm Ernst zu Fürstenberg moved his seat from Stühlingen to Donaueschingen, the locality thereby becoming "capital" of the **principality of Fürstenberg**. However, Donaueschingen has been able to call itself a town only since 1810.

The **palace** has been a **Belle Epoche residence** since undergoing a basic conversion in 1893-96. The magnificent reception and representation rooms of the princes' family can be **viewed**. Their precious furniture, paintings and art treasures give an impression of a grand life.

The **architecture** in Donaueschingen is a mixture of old and new. With the centralisation of the Fürstenberg administration in the 18th c. there was a great deal of building in **baroque style**. Examples of this, apart from the palace, are the **town church St. Johann with its twin towers**, the **archive, library, as** well as the former administration and *residential and servants' houses*.

Major events in Donaueschingen today are the equestrian tournament in September and the music festival in October.

Interior of prince's palace

Stairwell in prince's palace

Here in Titisee-Neustadt we see the fools' fountain and St. Jakobus-kirche.

The Titisee-Neustadt spa gardens underlines the town's reputation as the most attractive holiday spot in Baden-Württemberg.

Titisee-Neustadt

Titisee-Neustadt (12,000 inh.) comprises the districts **Titisee**, **Neustadt**, **Waldau**, **Langenordnach**, **Schwärzenbach** and **Rudenberg**. **Neustadt**, the **largest district**, was founded as customs and government office of the **princes zu Fürstenberg** in the 13th c. This locality, which had grown rich thanks to its forest, was granted a town charter in 1398. Old documents indicate how the name Neustadt developed from **Nova Civitas** via **Neuwenstadt**, **Neostadium** and **New-Statt**.

The hotel **"Adler-Post"**, which today still bears the Austrian eagle and Austrian colours as inn sign, was **Anterior Austrian post office** from 1516 and later office of the Thurn-und-Taxis-Post. The era of the mail coaches ended with the opening of the **Höllental railway** in 1887. Neustadt, which has been carefully refurbished, has preserved its **small town charm**.

The **Hochfirst**, rising up **1,190 metres**, is located between Neustadt and Titisee. In 2001 the first **World Cup Ski-Jumping took place in the Black Forest at** the **Hochfirst-schanze**, the largest **natural ski jumping hill in Germany**, during which **Sven Hannawald** jumped 145 metres, the jumping hill record. The first Hochfirst jumping hill was built in 1932. A larger ski-jumping hill was set up in 1950 and continually improved, the last time in 2001.

View of Hochfirstschanze

The **oldest district** of Titisee-Neustadt is **Waldau**. The founding of St. Peter monastery was mentioned for the first time in 1178 in a papal document. The **Waldauer Höfe** were hereditary estates of the monastery. The **Kreutz brothers** built one of the first Black Forest clocks, a **horizontal clock** running on three wooden wheels with only one hand, at the **Glashof** in Waldau in 1664.

It's time for refreshments in the rest house at a height of 1,188 metres.

The Hochfirst, 1,118 metres high, is a popular excursion destination for young and old.
Anyone who makes it up to the lofty heights is rewarded with a grandiose view of the Titisee.

Fountain Dengelebrunnen in Lenzkirch

Lenzkirch

The **spa and winter sport locality Lenzkirch (4,900 inh.)** is located in a valley basin of the Haslach. The medieval **castle ruins Alt-Urach** are among the oldest witnesses of the past. The later Princes von Fürstenberg came to power in 1491. The rustic **Schwendekapelle St. Cyriak**, probably the **oldest little church** in the surroundings, was for a long time destination of the **field processions** starting from Lenzkirch. The lake **Ursee** above Lenzkirch is located in a **nature reserve** with many rare plants. The **Moorsee**, which is cold and mostly filled up by sedimentation, is a relict from the Ice Age. An important date in the event calendar is the annual **Elogiusritt** in June, connected with a **fair**.

ruins Alt-Urach

Titisee

A nice legend has it that Titisee owes its name to the **Roman general Titus**. When he passed through the High Black Forest with his legions in the 1st c. AD, he is said to have been so taken with the beauty of the natural lake that he spontaneously gave the lake his name. The books of documents of the neighbouring parish **Saig**, where the names **Dettesee** and Titinsee are noted in 1111, are a more reliable source. The name **Titisee** became usual from 1750.

A hundred years ago there were only a handful of farmsteads at Titisee. The scattered settlement was called **"Viertäler"** up to 1929. Today Titisee is a **high-altitude health resort** with numerous hotels and guest-houses. It was combined with Neustadt, five km away, to form Titisee-Neustadt under the community reform.

The tourist infrastructure of Titisee includes a **spa centre**, **well-signposted network of foot-paths** and **open-air and bathing place** direct on the lake. The Titisee freezes over in winter and becomes an ice rink. A large **network of cross-country skiing courses**, **ski runs** and 1.2 km long **toboggan run** on the high Hochfirst are also provided for winter sports fans.

The Titisee is a former **moraine waters**. It was left behind by the former **Bärengletscher** glacier at the **Feldberg** as a natural artificial lake at the end of the last Ice Age. With its length of two km and width of 700 metres, Titisee is the **largest natural**

Enjoyable sea trip on the Titisee, which is 2 km long

lake in the Black Forest. The lake, approx. **40 metres deep**, is located in a very beautiful setting at a **height of 858 metres** between wooded slopes with the Feldberg-Massiv on one side and the Hochfirst on the other. The lake also obtains its water from the Feldberg. The **Seebach**, the drain of the **Feldsee**, flows through the Titisee, where the stream changes its name: it flows into the lake as Seebach and leaves it as **Gutach**. After joining the **Haslach**, the Seebach becomes near Lenzkirch the **Wutach**, which finally

Centre of the locality

flows into the Rhine at **Waldshut-Tiengen**. The lake is a nature reserve. Numerous types of fish flourish in its crystal-clear water. **Pike** over 1.20 metres long have been caught in the lake.

The Titisee is a very popular **destination** for **excursions** offering many types of water sport: **bathing**, **fishing**, **rowing**, **sailing** and **surfing**. There are also **excursion boats** and pedal boats on the lake.

Since having been redesigned into a **lake promenade** free of traffic, the Seestrasse is regarded as the most beautiful boulevard in the Southern Black Forest.

Hikers can use a well-laid path to walk around the lake in one and half hours. The **"water route"** is rather special: this **nature instruction path**, five km long, provides 16 information panels at 16 stations.

It´s worthwhile taking an excursion from Titisee to the **Jostal**. Along with its five western tributaries **Schildwende**, **Siedelbach**, **Eckbach**, **Bruckbach** and **Einsiedel**, this forms a valley landscape as if out of a

The local spa centre, the main task of which is to provide information about everything important for visitors.

Seestrasse in the evening

picture book. Jostal and Schild-wende belong to the town Titisee-Neustadt and the other valleys to the neighbouring **Breitnau**. There is a **baroque church** (1731) in the small spa **Friedenweiler** near Titisee-**Schollach**, a district of the health resort **Eisenbach**. Remains of this ski lift, which was in operation between 1906 and 1917, are still preserved. There is also a **bird museum** in Eisenbach.

View over the wintry Titisee showing the unique location of the health resorta

Neustadt. This belonged to a monas-tery, which after its closure served the Prince zu Fürstenberg as hunting lodge and summer seat. The **world's oldest skilift** is said to have been in

You can really feel the cold of the snow-draped landscape!

Hinterzarten

The **climatic spa and winter sport locality Hinterzarten (2,600 inh.)** used to be called **"Hinter der Strass"**, Breitnau in the north being called "Vor der Strass". The name Hinterzarten occurs between 1708 and 1750. The **Zartenbach** probably gave the church and the locality its name. **Black Forest ski museum** in **Hugenhof**. **Adler-Skistadion** with its four ramps can be used as a training centre for ski jumpers all year round.

It is worth seeing the Catholic church, the **foundation stone** of which was laid in 1460. The **tower**, **choir** and

Adler-Skistadion with its four ramps can be used as a training centre for ski jumpers all year round.

The place is well-known as the home of the famous ski jumper **Georg Thoma** and his nephew **Dieter Thoma**. Their successes and the over 100-year history of skiing sport in the Black Forest are documented in the

baroque altars remained preserved during all the conversions and extensions. The former **nave** was demolished and replaced by a very modern **octagonal hall**. The **oldest building** is the St. Oswaldkapelle from the 12th c. The **Jockeleshofmühle**, built in the 19th c., has as special feature a single **water-wheel** driving a **milling plant** and a **saw**.

The enormous **Ice Age glaciers** have left **lakes** around Hinterzarten that have almost all been filled up by sedimentation. **Hinterzartener Moor** is regarded as one of the best preserved **high moors** in Central Europe.

Magnificent parish church Maria in the Zarten in winter

One of the many romantic home-steads that are typical of the Black Forest.

Agriculture

Picturesque Scattered picturesque farmsteads set amidst meadows and forests: that's the Black Forest. The attractive changes between green meadows and dark fields are what make the Black Forest so unique. Preserving this landscape is one of the most important tasks of the local farmers.

And yet many of the steep areas of the valleys were afforested because they could otherwise be cultivated only laboriously by hand. Forest meanwhile covers over 90 percent of the area of quite a few communities. Promotional programmes and grazing concepts are to halt this trend. Often a second source of income helps to secure the future of a farm. Self-marketing with baking bread, distilling schnapps and producing meat for the farm's own shop has become important. The popular **"holidays on the farm"** are also a good source of additional income.

These picturesque scenes belong more to the past in the Black Forest, as elsewhere.

A distant bleating is carried over by the wind from the herd of sheep.

Höllental and Ravennaschlucht

The king of the forest majestically surveying the Höllental

The **walls of rock** rising steeply up to **600 metres high** narrowing one of the most impressive Black Forest valleys must have reminded former travellers of hell and so they called it **Höllental** (Hell Valley).

The story of the **Stag's Leap**, the narrowest part of the valley, has also always fired the imagination. Proudly perched high up on the rock, a **stag of bronze** recalls that at this place a member of the same species, undaunted by death, once saved itself from hunters by taking an enormous leap over the gorge. Anyone who considers this story to be a fable should bear in mind that since the legendary stag's leap the gorge has been widened several times at this point for road-building.

Up to 200 years ago there was only a narrow **mule track** in the gorge about ten km long along the **Rotbach**. This was then expanded into a roadway. Today the route through the Höllental is an important **connecting road** from the Rhine plain into the Southern Black Forest.

In 1770, the old roadway was also taken by the Austrian **Empress's daughter Marie-Antoinette** when travelling to France to join her bridegroom, the later King Louis XVI. The area was at that time **Austrian**.

A ramble through very impressive landscape leads on the ten km long **hunters' path** from Hinterzarten through the Höllental down to **Himmelreich**, just before Kirchzarten.

At **Höllsteig**, the wildly romantic **Ravenna Gorge** flows into the Höllental. The little river **Ravenna** plunges from the plateau near Breitnau as **waterfalls** 200 metres down into the ravine. The ravine is accessible by steps and galleries. The **Heimatpfad**, along a hiking route passing **Black Forest mills**, also goes through it. At the lower exit, the Höllental railway crosses over the **Ravenna Viaduct**. With its length of 222 metres and height of 42 metres, this is the most impressive structure of the Höllental railway.

Wildly romantic Ravenna Gorge

Höllsteig

Hofgut Sternen

The domain Hofgut **Sternen** in **Höllsteig** at the upper end of the Höllental once even had the famous German writer **Johann Wolfgang Goethe** as guest. The **chapel St. Oswald** is a jewel. It was consecrated in **1148** and is one of the oldest places of worship in the Black Forest. The late Gothic altar dates from 1518.

Ravenna Viaduct with Hofgut Sternen in the foreground

Höllental railway

The **Höllental railway** is one of the most interesting rail routes in Germany. The rail route, opened in **1887** by **Grand Duke Friedrich I**, runs largely parallel to the present federal highway. It led initially to Titisee-Neustadt. It has linked **Freiburg** with **Donaueschingen** since 1901.

The locomotives have to overcome a **gradient** of over **600 metres** on the steep stretch between Himmelreich at the entrance of the Höllental and Hinterzarten on the plateau. The technically difficult route was planned by the railway pioneer **Robert Gerwig**, builder of the Black Forest railway. He designed nine tunnels and some viaducts.

The trip with the Höllental railway used to be slow. Up to 1933 only **cogwheel locomotives** could run on the steep section at a speed of 30 km per hour. Today the train manages the ascent twice as fast.

Kirchzarten

The Celts once settled on the communal district of *Kirchzarten (9,000 inh.)*. The fortifications are partially still visible, partially proven by archaeological research. A **church** was mentioned in **"Zartunu"** for the first time in 816. The present **parish church St. Gallus** is largely a Gothic building from the 18th c. In the interior there is also the **gravestone** of the **knight Kuno von Falkenstein**, who died in 1363.

Fools' fountain in Kirchzarten

Freiburg im Breisgau

Freiburg (221,400 inh.), university town and cultural centre of the Breisgau, is a major centre that has nevertheless retained a great deal of small town charm. It is located in Dreisamtal between the **Southern Black Forest** and **Kaiserstuhl** and has a **very mild climate**.

Nature and the environment have had a high priority in Freiburg – and not since the very first green mayor has been in office in the town hall. The town is exemplary in its use of solar energy.

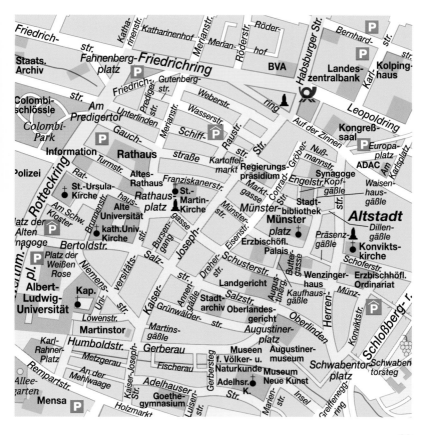

History of Freiburg

After the **Zähringer** built a castle on the **Schlossberg** in 1091, they raised

the smaller settlements in the area of the present southern **old town** and **Oberlinden** to the status of town in 1120. The Zähringer were followed by the **counts of Freiburg**. In 1368 the citizens bought themselves off from their rule with a high one-off payment and voluntarily put themselves under the powerful **House of Habsburg**.

In the 19th c., Freiburg developed into an economic and political centre on the east side of the upper Rhine. It became a **bishop's seat** in 1821. The **first train** went from the new Freiburg station to Offenburg in 1845. New districts, the **Wiehre** and **Stühlinger**, were created.

The **town theatre** was inaugurated in 1910. In 1920 and 1921, the Reich President appointed the Freiburg citizens Konstantin Fehrenbach and Joseph Wirth Reich Chancellors. Large parts of the town were destroyed in an **air raid** on **November 27th 1944**. Since the amalgamation of Baden with Württemberg in 1952, Freiburg has been seat of the top government body for South Baden.

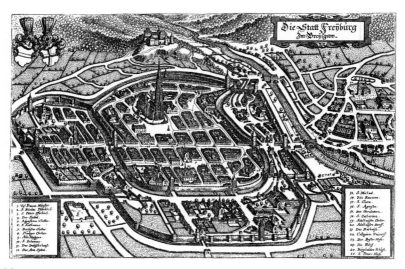

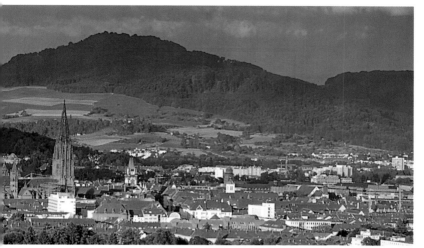

The Zähringer town of Freiburg, gateway to the Southern Black Forest

Freiburger minster

The spire **116 metres high** with the perforated pyramid-shaped top over the roofs of the old town points the way to the **minster Unserer Lieben Frau**. It was completed around **1330** and regarded as an architectural marvel. Berthold V, the last Zähringer duke, began building the church in **late Romanesque style** around 1200. Some decades later, **French Gothic** served as model. The plans were changed several times during the construction work, and the town church became a cathedral.

However, Freiburg overtaxed itself with the project, and the building of the choir came to a standstill in 1370. Construction activity was resumed only a century later.

Freiburg minster, one of the largest buildings in Germany

The numerous gargoyles have an impressive variety of designs.

91

View of altar

Statue of Mary in Gothic style

Gothic rose window in the northern nave

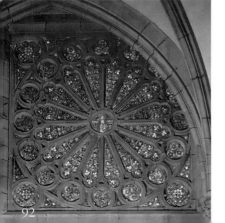

The bishop of Konstanz Hugo consecrated the church in 1513, when most of it was completed. The **outer facades** of the minster have many **adornments**, including **gargoyles** and **stone figures** of the apostles, kings, counts and saints, although many of the figures are damaged or concealed behind scaffolding. The **sandstone** used in the construction was not very weather-proof, and parts of the spire were frequently torn down in thunderstorms. The minster was also continually damaged in the wars of the past centuries.

The **church rooms** are particularly beautiful on sunny days when the **colourful glass windows** come into their own. Most of them were created around 1320, donated by the wealthy Freiburg **guilds and miners**. The Kaiser Maximilian window designs are of **imperial eagles** and **coats of arms** of the areas ruled by the Habsburgs. **Hans Baldung Grien** created the famous pictures of the high altar between 1512 and 1516. The fourfold organ consists of the gallery, nave, Virgin Mary and choir organ.

The **oldest of the minster bells** is the **Hosianna** from 1258. Its sombre tone recalls the crucifixion of Christ every **Friday at eleven**.

The parsonage was on the **Münster-platz** up to the 18th c. There is colourful **market bustle** there on weekdays.

Sights

Münsterplatz is lined by several historic buildings. The shining **red department store** with **oriels**, **arcade** and **stepped gable** (1532) was built as trading centre for foreign merchants. The **corn store** (15th c.) with the beautiful **stepped gable** was rebuilt in its original form after the second world war. The late Gothic **fish fountain** was installed in front of the corn store.

The Freiburg **town gates** are also well-known. The **Martinstor**, originally called Norsinger Tor, on Kaiser-Joseph-Strasse, the **oldest** preserved **defensive and gate tower** of the medieval fortifications, dates from the beginning of the 13th c. It was raised from 21 to 63 metres at the beginning of the 20th c. The **Schwabentor** (1250) with its pointed arches has a **pewter figure workshop** and shop in its upper floor.

Corn store on Münsterplatz
Historic department store (1520)

Schwabentor (13th c.) at the end of Salzstrasse

The traditional university, still important today

University

When Freiburg passed from Anterior Austria to Baden in 1805, the university, founded in **1457** by **Archduke Albrecht VI**, initially faced an uncertain future. Grand Duke **Ludwig von Baden** then ensured its continuance in 1820, so the university called itself after the two aristocrats **Albert-Ludwigs-Universität** (Albert being the Latin form of Albrecht).

Even at its founding in 1457, the university could offer courses in theology, law, medicine and philosophy. With the influx of students in the 19th c., the university soon expanded out of its medieval walls. Freiburg university matriculated the **first woman in Germany** in **1899**. Today the university has over **21,500 students**.

Apart from its university, Freiburg has a state university for music, college of education and Catholic as well as a Protestant college for social studies.

The research institutions **Fraunhofer**- and **Max-Planck-Gesellschaft** are also based in Freiburg.

Houses/leisure

The traditional **Zum Roten Bären** on the square **Oberlinden** is one of Germany´s **oldest inns**. The line of publicans managing this inn can be traced without interruption back to 1387. The **baroque fountain Marienbrunnen** murmurs under a lime tree planted in 1729.

One of the most beautiful middle-class houses is the **Haus zum Walfisch** (1516) near the Martinskirche with its artistically forged gate and a late Gothic oriel.

The **nature and ethnology museum** in the former **Adelhausen Monastery** has interesting and important collections. The new **planetarium** offers a fascinating view of the starry sky. The preserve **Mundenhof** in the district **Lehen** is a popular destination for family excursions.

Haus zum Walfisch, one of the most beautiful houses in Freiburg

Oberlinden at night – the people of Freiburg like going out

Inn Zum roten Bären

Freiburg "Bächle"

Streamlets

A speciality of Freiburg are the streamlets, **"Bächle"**. Originally they were probably intended for supplying **industrial water** and serving as **canals for sewage**. Today the watercourses in the old town ensure a pleasant **climate** and are a **playground** for people of all ages. Anyone who inadvertently ever gets wet feet can console themselves: in Freiburg one says that **anyone who steps into a streamlet has not been in the town for the last time**.

Freiburg´s local hill, Schauinsland

Schauinsland, 1,284 metres high, is Freiburg's **local hill**. As the name ("Look into the Land") suggests, a magnificent panoramic view is offered from the top and lookout tower of the hill. Schauinsland is accessible via a **winding hill road** and a **cable car**. The **valley station** of the mountain railway is located high up in **Horben** above Freiburg.

If the visibility is good, there is an impressive view from Schauinsland of the massive Alps.

A typical feature of Schauinsland are the extensive meadows on its plateau created after **clearings** in the Middle Ages to obtain wood needed for **mining**. The Schauinsland used to be called **"Erzkasten"** ("Ore Chest") on account of its **mineral wealth**. The 14th and 15th c. was the heyday of mining. **Silver, lead and zinc** were mined. Tunnels with an overall length of 100 km were dug over the years. In the interior of Schauinsland there is the **largest silver mine** in the Black Forest with 22 floors. It has been a public **mine for visitors** since 1997.

Schauinsland cableway

The old town hall of Lahr seems embedded in roses.

The historic town centre of Ettenheim, protected as an historic monument

Ettenheim

The centre of **Ettenheim (11,800 inh.)** is protected as an **historic monument**. The narrow lanes are lined with baroque buildings and half-timbered houses from the 17th and 18th c., which was the heyday of the little town, founded in the 8th c.

by an **Alemannian ducal dynasty**. Two gates remain of the former **town fortifications**. The **town church St. Bartholomäus** (1777) in the centre of Ettenheim has the **grave** of the Strasbourg cardinal **Louis de Rohan** (1734-1803), who fled over the Rhine during the French Revolution and found his last place of refuge in Ettenheim. **Palais Rohan** is opposite the **town hall** (1757) with its bell tower. The former **pilgrimage church St. Lanolin** in the district **Ettenheimmünster** has a bust of the saint (1508) with a relic and also a **Silbermann organ**.

Lahr

Lahr (43,500 inh.) has to thank the lords of Geroldseck for its creation. A settlement developed around the **moated castle** (early 13th c.) that received a town charter in 1279. The **Storchenturm** in the pedestrian zone is the only memory of this castle. Sights in the old town centre include the **old town hall**, a Renaissance building (1608) with arcades and a little belfry. The **Burgheim church** (1035) is one of the oldest churches in Baden. The beautiful town park, a legacy of the Lahr citizen Christian Wilhelm Jamm (1809-75) has **old exotic trees**. Lahr becomes really colourful in late autumn when the leaves fall. During the **"Chrysanthema"** thousands of chrysanthemums adorn the lanes, square, fountains and houses in the pedestrian zone as hanging cascades or bushes.

Europapark Rust

Europapark in **Rust**, **Germany's largest leisure park**, attracts more and more visitors every year. The area has been enlarged several times since its opening in a **palace park** in 1975. Europapark meanwhile has over a hundred attractions. **Sheer thrills** are offered by roller coasters such as the **"Silver Star"**, 73 metres high and thus Europe's highest **steel roller coaster**. The park is divided up into various subject areas sponsored by European countries. Sights are the former **Russian space station Mir** and a replica of the original **Shakespearean theatre**. Entertainment includes knightly tournaments, gladiator stunts, an ice revue and a 4D cinema.

Emmendingen

The centre of the county town **Emmendingen (26,100 inh.)** is the **market place**, from which all the streets radiate. Some fine old middle-class houses are noticeable features. The town, mentioned for the first time in 1094, became the **seat of a margrave** at the end of the 16th c.

The **old cemetery** has the grave of Goethe's sister **Cornelia Schlosser** (1750-77), who died young. She lived in the town with her husband, the administrator of a margrave, and was visited by her famous brother.

Emmendingen's sights include the **town hall** (1729), built on the market square on the walls of a medieval **community and court room**. The **late Gothic choir** of the Protestant town church still shows that it was

Emmendingen market place, an attractive mixture of fine middle-class houses and Gothic town church

built at the end of the 15th c. The **palace** of the margraves of Baden, a simple Renaissance building (1585), has a **local history museum**. The association for **Jewish history and culture** has also set up a small museum.

Good vintages from sunny vineyard slopes

Grape harvest

No one can say no to a little tot.

The wine state of Baden stretches over 400 km from the lower **Tauber Valley** up the Rhine to **Lake Constance**. With its approx. 16,000 ha of vineyards, it is the third largest of the 13 German viticulture regions. The heart of Baden viticulture is formed by the regions located on the sun-soaked western edge of the Black Forest **Ortenau**, **Breisgau**, **Kaiserstuhl** with **Tuniberg** and **Markgräflerland**. The most important types of grape are Müller-Thurgau, Spätburgunder, Riesling, Grauburgunder and Gutedel.

The **Romans** brought viticulture to Baden long ago. It is attested that at **Kaiserstuhl** vines have been planted since **769**. Viticulture was promoted from the 18th c. by the mediatized princes and monasteries, particularly Karl Friedrich von Baden (1728-1811). The first **winegrowers' cooperative** in Baden was founded in 1881 by the pastor and regional writer **Heinrich Hansjakob** (1837-1916) in Hagnau on Lake Constance. The first winegrowers' cooperatives at the Kaiserstuhl were founded in 1924.

Kaiserstuhl

The **Kaiserstuhl**, 16 km long and 12 km wide with the 557 metres high **death's head** at its summit, rises like an island out of the Upper Rhine Plain. The **volcanic massif** was created about 16 million years ago. The fertile loess soils and the mild climate benefit viticulture. The Kaiserstuhl is one of the **warmest areas** in Germany. The small stepped terraced vineyards and the **narrow passes** between them used to be typical for it. The region now has **extensive terraces** following the not uncontroversial reallocations of arable land in the 1970s.

View up to the death's head, 557 metres high

Bahlingen

Bahlingen (3,700 inh.) was mentioned for the first time in **762** in the will of the bishop Eto of Strasbourg. The **old village centre** has many typical Kaiserstuhl **winegrower houses** with stone cellar and ground floors and half-timbering in the upper floor. The **church tower** dates from 1408.

Riegel

Riegel (3,600 inh.) is located on the **northern edge of the Kaiserstuhl**. It was mentioned for the first time in 763 as **"Rigola"**, but was already a prestigious settlement in **Roman times**. Finds from the Bronze Age and Celtic and Roman times have been preserved in the town hall. The baroque **parish church St. Martin** features two **Madonnas** from the 15th c. The Michaelskapelle also dates from this time.

Riegeler town hall

The town of Endingen with its medieval romantic atmosphere

Endingen

Endingen (9,000 inh.) is one of the most beautiful localities in the Kaiserstuhl. Its origins go back to an **Alemannian settlement** mentioned in 763. Endingen was given a town charter in 1290. Its old **half-timbered houses** date from the 16th and 17th c. Of the town gates, **Königsschaffhauser Tor** has remained. The former corn store (1617) with its stepped gable, now seat of the community administration, is on the **market square**. There is a **museum** in the old town hall.

101

Sasbach

Sasbach (3,300 inh.) was located direct on the **Rhine** until 1850 and its inhabitants were **fisherfolk**. Since the correction of the river, which is now a kilometre away, the people of Sasbach have engaged in viticulture. The **church St. Martin** (1741) with its **Romanesque belfry** and baroque high altar as well as the **ruins of Limburg castle**, a former Zähringer castle, are worth seeing.

Achkarren

Achkarren, which has formed the town **Vogtsburg (5,800 inh.)** with

Achkarren, surrounded by vines

six other traditional **wine-growing localities** since the community reform in 1975, is the **heart of the Kaiserstuhl** and the largest winegrowing community in Baden-Württemberg. The Kaiserstuhl **viticulture museum in Achkarren** is also concerned with the juice of the grape.

Ihringen

Nowhere in Germany does the sun shine for so many hours as in **Ihrin-**

gen (5,800 inh.). This winegrowing community is also regarded as the **warmest place in Germany**. Celtic and Roman finds indicate that the settlement is the **oldest** in the **Kaiserstuhl**. According to old documents, Ihringen was already a considerable winegrowing community in 962.

Burkheim

Burgheim on the **western edge of the Kaiserstuhl** today also belongs to the town Vogtsburg. This locality, which dates from 762, had its heyday from the 16th c. Narrow little lanes and streets lead from the lower to the upper town.

Burkheim town gate

Breisach: the minster St. Stephan dominating the Rhine

Breisach

The **Münsterberg** dominating the town used to be a continual source of trouble for the **"Europe town" Breisach (14,000 inh.)**. Even the Romans appreciated the outstanding strategic significance of **"Mons Brisiacus"** and built a **fortress** on it. From the 10th c., Breisach developed into one of the most important localities on the Upper Rhine. In 1198 Duke Berthold V. of Zähringen began with the construction of a mighty **castle** on the Berg and a **large well**, 42 metres deep. Breisach showed its wealth by building the minster St. Stephan from 12th-15th c., which accommodates precious works of art: a **high altar** carved of limewood, a silver reliquary and the wall painting **"Das Jüngste Gericht"** ("The Last Judgment") by **Martin Schongauer**. In 1793, **Empress Maria Theresia**, eager to put an end to the eternal bone of contention between Germany and France, had the town's enormous fortifications razed. Fifty years later, French revolutionary troops destroyed the town that had grown over the centuries. Breisach remained a **town of ruins** until into the early 19th c.

The **town centre** moved into the **lower town**, while **vineyards** were created on the hill. Breisach and the Münster were severely damaged again in spring 1945.

There is a **theatre festival** on a open-air stage in Breisach **between June and September**. The museum steam train **"Rebenbummler"** (slow train through the vines) goes between Breisach and Riegel. At the port, **excursion ships** depart on round trips on the Rhine.

Breisach also has the **Badischer Winzerkeller**, one of the largest winegrowing businesses in the state.

Bad Krozingen

Bad Krozingen (15,600 inh.) was originally an **Alemannian settlement**. Its name **"Scrozzinga"** was mentioned for the first time in a deed of donation issued in **808** for St. Gallen Monastery. The rule over the locality, which belonged to the Anterior Austrian landgraviate Breisgau up to 1805, changed several times over the centuries.

Krozingen's development as **spa**

Lammplatz in Bad Krozingen

and bathing place dates from the **thermal spring** bubbling metres high discovered during drillings in **1911**. The **39.40°** warm medicinal water is not only rich in minerals: it has one of the highest **concentrations of carbonic acid** in the whole of Europe – 2200 mg per litre. The first spa guests bathed in it in 1913. Since 1933 the community has been allowed to add **"Bad"** ("Bath") to its name. It now has clinics in addition to **movement baths** and **therapy facilities**.

The **Vita Classica thermal baths**, an elegant bathing palace with a **classical atmosphere**, was opened in **1995**. It offers six basins with **700 m2 of water area** inside and outside.

Concerts of music from the 16th-19th c. are held in the **festive hall** decorated with stucco of the **palace**, a former **provostry** of St. Blasien Monastery. The complex, built in 1579, also accommodates a **collection** of about **50 instruments** built **between 1600 and 1860**, including positive organs, spinets, spinettinos, virginals, harpsichords, clavichords, tangent action pianos, square pianofortes and exquisite pianofortes, illustrating the development of **piano construction** over four centuries. The **palace chapel** is designed in rococo style.

Another sight is the **Glöcklehof Chapel** with its old murals from the 10th c. in the district **Ober-Krozingen**.

The Vita Classica thermal baths, ideal for relaxation

The domed hall of the Vita Classica thermal baths certainly makes you want to go bathing.

Staufen

Staufen (7,700 inh.), a little town located at the entrance to the **Münster valley**, has a beautiful **historic centre**. This locality, known for winegrowing and the distilling of fine fruit spirits, dates back to 707. The settlement developed under the protection of **Staufen Castle**, built

"... no kirschwasser without cherries"

The little town of Staufen where Faust lived is known for its wines as well as its high-proof spirits distilled from fruit.

on a **mountain cone** at the beginning of the 12th c. Staufen was granted a town charter in 1280.

The car-free **town centre** has attractive nooks and lanes and houses from the 17th and 18th c. **The town hall on the market place** dates from 1546. The exhibits in the museum in **Stubenhaus** on the market square, one of the town's oldest buildings, recall the once flourishing **silver mining** in the region and the **"Battle of Staufen"** during the Baden revolution.

The life of a complex personality who passed into literature via Staufen is also documented: **Johannes Faust** (1480-1539), doctor, astrologist and alchemist. After the sudden death of the scholar, who

served the barons of Staufen, the legend arose that he had been taken by his masters. The inn **Zum Löwen**, the scene of the drama, devoted an inscription to him and a **"Faust room"**.

The parish church St. Martin has an interesting combination of modern high altar and **late Gothic crucifix**. The **ceramics museum** with a **potter's workshop** showing the development of the craft of pottery is also worth seeing.

If you walk up to the ruins of Staufen Castle, high up on a vineyard above the town, you'll be rewarded with a beautiful view.

Münstertal

Untermünstertal, which used to be known for silver mining

The health resort **Münstertal (5,000 inh.)** is scattered down a six km long valley at the foot of the **Belchen**. The oldest traces of **silver mining** date from the **11th c.** New findings show that a **mining town** was created in the 13th c. that was **buried** under an enormous **mudflow** at the beginning of the 15th c. Mining was resumed in the 18th c. and **lead** obtained up to **1864**. The beekeeping museum in Obermünstertal is worth seeing.

St. Trudpert Monastery, founded in 640, was built on the square where the Irish monk died a martyr's death.

Schönau

Schönau (2,500 inh.) in Wiesen Valley is a popular starting point for hiking expeditions to **Belchen**. The sights of the **health resort**, mentioned for the first time in 1202, are the **parish church** (1890) and **town hall**. The picture of a saint with the power to work miracles in the little **pilgrimage church Schönenbuchen** features angels wearing local traditional costume.

Belchen

The **Belchen**, with a height of **1,414 metres** the **third highest mountain** in the Black Forest, offers one of the most beautiful **views** of the region.

The Belchen has its striking silhouette to thank for its name – in **Alemannian**, **dome-shaped hills without trees** were called "Belchen". The Black Forest Belchen therefore also has large and small brothers in Alsace and Switzerland. However, the **Celtic sun god Belenos** could also have inspired the name, as traces of **cult sites** have been discovered on all these hills.

The Belchen, the **second largest granite massif** apart from the Feldberg, has remarkable **flora and fauna**. In the high areas there are many rare species of butterfly, beetle and bird.

Schönau can be a beautiful starting point for hikes into Wiesen Valley.

The hiking area around the Belchen is one of the most popular excursion destinations in the entire Black Forest.

Belchenhaus near the top is also a hotel.

The cable railway operates all year round, in summer and winter.

On clear days you can see as far as the Alps.

Song thrushes, citril finches and water pipits, as well as **peregrine falcons**, **wood grouse** and **hazel hens** are to be found here.

Belchen's many plants, such as the **Swiss bluebell**, **Alpine dogrose** and **Swiss dandelion**, that are otherwise to be found almost only in the Alps are relics of the Ice Age.

Because of its special flora and fauna, the Belchen has been protected since 1949. Following its extension in 1993, the **Belchen nature reserve** covering 1,600 ha is one of the largest in Baden Württemberg.

Belchenstrasse was the first summit road in the Black Forest to be completely closed off (since 1990). The top can be conveniently reached by a gondola lift, opened in 2001. Its construction was the prerequisite for the Belchen being freed from all traffic. There are steep hiking routes leading through a very attractive landscape from the **Münster** and **Wiesen Valley** up the mountain.

Todtnau

The **health resort Todtnau (5,200 inh.)** was mentioned as **"Tote Aue"** for the first time in a document in the 12th c. The locality of Todtnau in the **Upper Wiesen Valley** is popular among hikers and winter sports fans alike. The **first skiing club** was

Market square of Todtnau

Todtnau waterfalls, 100 metres high, is accessible from the district Todtnauberg

founded here in Germany in 1891. Near the **Notschrei-Pass**, the **Stübenbach** plunges as wildly romantic **waterfalls** down 94 metres.

Feldberg

The **Feldberg, 1,494 metres high**, is the **highest mountain** in Black Forest. The weather conditions on the peak are accordingly bleak. The **annual average temperature** is

close on 4°, and there is a lot of rain and snow. The flatly domed summit of the Bergkönig is above the **tree line**. In the north-east the plateau descends almost vertically. At the foot of the wall is the **Feldsee**, a cirque, which the **Feldberg glacier** dug out in the last Ice Age.

The "Highest", as the Feldberg is respectfully called, is a paradise for skiers in winter.

Feldsee, one of the Ice Age lakes in the Black Forest

Valley station with gondola

A **cable car** runs between **Feldberger Hof** and **Seebuck** below the top. The **Bismarck monument**, built of granite blocks in 1896, is next to the hill station. There is a **broadcasting tower** on the summit. **Skiers** can choose between various courses, from the **beginner's** to the **World Cup course**. The skiing areas Seebuck, Grafenmatt and Fahl Alpin with a total of over **25 km of courses** and **twelve lifts** are direct

on the massif. There are numerous foot-paths and over **60 km of cross-country skiing courses**.

However, the Feldberg area is more than a holiday area. The Feldberg is not only the **oldest nature reserve** in Baden-Württemberg (since 1937) but also the largest. It is looked after by the **Black Forest rangers**.

The flora on the Feldberg is unique, an example being the **Alpine soldanel**, a relict from the Ice Age. There are **chamois** in the direction of Stollenbach/Zastler. The **Southern Black Forest Nature Protection Centre** was opened at Feldberg in 2001. The **"House of Nature"** informs visitors about the landscape and people and the flora and fauna with a permanent exhibition as well as a programme with guided tours, seminars and lectures.

If you come by rail, you arrive in **Bärental**, the **second highest station** in Germany. The station of the **Dreiseenbahn** is at a height of 967 metres.

The locality Bärental was mentioned as early as 1691. Along with Feldberg-Ort, **Altglashütten**, **Falkau** and **Neuglashütten**, it forms the community **Feldberg (1,800 inh.)**.

Bismarck monument on the Feldberg, 1,494 metres above sea level

A comprehensive network of cross-country skiing courses links up many communities in higher locations in the Black Forest.

Most of the **skiing areas** for Alpine and cross-country skiing are located at higher altitudes in the mountainous areas of the Southern Black Forest: in Belchenland, the holiday region around Schönwald and Schonach, the Todtnau holiday region and, of course, the Feldberg area. In the Northern Black Forest the winter sports venues are located along the Black Forest high road.

Many winter sport venues also have **toboggan runs**. The Todtnauer Bahn is the longest with a length of over three km. Triberg and Saig provide floodlighting. Skaters have a large number of outdoor and indoor ice rinks to choose from, including Bad Dürrheim, Bad Liebenzell, Baiersbronn, Bühl-Sand, Donaueschingen, Herrischried, Offenburg, Triberg, Schönwald, St. Georgen, Villingen-Schwenningen and Waldbronn. When temperatures fall below freezing, lakes and ponds also become ice-skating venues, the largest being Titisee.

Just too beautiful – a sleigh ride through the snowed-up winter forest

Energetically negotiating deep snow or swiftly wedeling – skiing is a really thrilling sport.

Windgfällweiher, also one of the Ice Age lakes

Altglashütten

Altglashütten, a district of the **community Feldberg**, was founded in 1634 as a **glass-making factory**. In 1669 the princes zu Fürstenberg sold the houses to the 40 glass-making families living there, thus creating a place that is popular today thanks to its good air and quiet atmosphere. **Neuglashütten** is also a **natural oasis** on the **long-distance skiing route**.

Around Schluchsee

Schluchsee, the **largest Black Forest lake**, is an artificial lake at a height of over 900 metres. It is 7.5 km long, about 1.5 km wide and up to 60 metres deep. Schluchsee was originally a much smaller **glacial lake**. A masonry dam, 35 metres high and 250 metres wide, was installed in 1932 near **Seebrugg**, causing the lake to expand. The dammed water is used to **generate electricity**. It is gradually led over 25 km to the High Rhine, approx. 600 metres deeper. There are **power stations** generating electricity at every barrage weir with lock.

With its masonry dam, Schluchsee is the largest lake in the Black Forest.

Schluchsee is a popular area for **water sports fans** with sufficient wind for **surfing and sailing**. **Schluchsee village** offers a **bathing place** as well as a **fun pool**. The 20 km long **path around the lake** is very attractive for exploring the area on foot or by bike.

The community **Schluchsee (2,600 inh.)**, a **climatic health resort**, consists of the districts **Aha**, **Blasi-wald**, **Faulenfürst**, **Fischbach-Hinterhäuser**, **Seebrugg**, **Schö-nenbach** and **Schluchsee-Ort**.

The first settlers in **Alb Valley** were mentioned in 1076, when Duke Rudolph of Rheinfelden donated the **"Landgut Schluchsee"** to St. Blasien Monastery. The actual founding of the locality Schluchsee began in 1083 with the first settle-ment of the **Bruderhof**, which was managed by lay brothers of the monastery.

Fog obscures the view over Schluch-see. One can only guess its size.

Grafenhausen

The most well-known building in **Grafenhausen (2,400 inh.)** is the handsome **museum of local history and culture Hüsli**, which

The museum of local history and culture Hüsli, made famous by the TV series "Black Forest Clinic" in Grafenhausen

became a TV star as residence of the professor family **Brinkmann** in the series **"Black Forest Clinic"**. The health resort Grafenhausen was founded in 1078. Another sight is the age-old **Tannenmühle**.

Bonndorf

Bonndorf (6,900 inh.) is known to nature lovers as the **starting point** for hikes in the famous Wutach gorge. A **13 km long tour** through the wildest part of the valley begins at nearby **Boll**. The ravine with its rare mosses, ferns, herbs, flowers, birds, butterflies and beetles has been under strict nature protection since 1928. The 16th c. **moated castle**, accommodating the **museum of the district Waldhut**, is worth seeing in Bonndorf.

Blumberg

Fans of **nostalgic railways** love **Blumberg (10,600 inh.)**, which has operated the 25 km long **train route**, built in 1890 as a "strategic railway" between **Blumberg-Zollhaus and Weizen**, as a **museum railway for steam trains** since 1977. The **"Sauschwänzlebahn"** has become a tourist attraction. The railway owes its original name to the way the tracks wind through the tunnels like a little pigtail.

The Sauschwänzlebahn between Blumberg and Stühlingen recalls the good old days of steam. The rail route, 28 km long, was completed in 1890.

Höchenschwand

Höchenschwand (2,400 inh.) is nicknamed **"Village in the Sky"**. Its beautiful location at a height of 1,015 metres, pure air, many hours of sunshine and magnificent **view** of the **Swiss Alps** have attracted visitors for over 100 years. The **inn Ochsen** from the 17th c. was converted in 1873 to become the village's first **spa facility**.

Höchenschwand, "Village in the Sky"

Häusern

The little **health resort** and **winter sport locality Häusern (1,300 inh.)** is located on the saddle between the two ravine-like valleys of **Alb** and **Schwarza**. A **hydro-electric power station** of the Schluchseewerke and the lake **Albtalstausee** are located below the locality. The Alb Valley is also known for its spectacular **waterfalls**.

Kandern power station

St. Blasien

St. Blasien (4,100 inh.), a climatic health resort with the districts **Albtal** and **Menzenschwand**, lies at the foot of the **Feldberg**. The unmistakeable **symbol** of the little town is the **cathedral** built between 1771 and 1783 with its dome 64 metres high. This building, modelled on the **Pantheon** in Rome, is regarded as one of the **largest domed buildings** in Europe and a **masterpiece** of **early classicism**. It was the work of the famous French architect Pierre Michel d'Ixnard. The builder was the monastery principal **Fürstabt Martin Gerbert**,

The cathedral in St. Blasien can be seen from far away – the third largest dome in Europe really seems to dominate everything.

Interior of the cathedral flooded with light

A look into Europe's third largest dome

(1720-1793), who wrote the **first documentation** on the Black Forest. The local school is named after him.

The **Benedictine monastery** of St. Blasien, whose origins go back to the 9th c., made an important contribution to the development of the **Black Forest**. The former **monastery building** today houses the **Kolleg St. Blasien**, a state-recognized **grammar school** under the **Jesuit order** with a **boarding school** for boys and girls that has educated various personalities from politics, culture and business.

St. Blasien's development as a **spa** began in **1877** when a doctor and a hotelier opened the first spa facility, a **lung sanatorium**. The beautifully sited spa gardens feature a **baroque sundial**.

The **backdrop of the magnificent cathedral is also occasionally used as stage** for **open-air theatre performances**. However, it has not yet been possible to make the cathedral festival a fixed component of the cultural programme as hoped. An **international sculptural competition** is regularly held in St. Blasien.

There are interesting walks to **Kalvarienberg**, **903 metres** high and offering a beautiful view of the town, and to **Hohfelsen** at the romantic **Windberg waterfalls**.

The beautiful, lovingly restored monastery buildings

The well-known spa Todtmoos with its newly created spa gardens has a relaxing atmosphere.

Todtmoos

Todtmoos (2,100 inh.) is located in the Upper **Wehra Valley**. The **health resort** is dominated by the baroque **pilgrimage church Mariä Himmelfahrt** on the **Schönbühl**. Pilgrims have come here since the 15th c. The priest Dietrich von Rickenbach built the first chapel in 1255. The name **"Toten Moos"** became "Todtmoos". The present **church** was newly designed and decorated in the 18th c. and expanded in 1927 with a new tower and two **side aisles**. Todtmoos used to belong to St. Blasien Monastery, which had the **parsonage** built in the 18th c.

The **centre** of the community is protected from the wind at the foot of the local hill, the **Hochkopf, 1,263 metres** high. The height of between 500 and 1200 metres usually ensures enough snow for **winter sports**. **Sledge dog races** also take place in late January. The huskies have already run twice for the **world championships** on the course in **Todtmoos-Schwarzenbach**.

The annual international sledge dog races are always an attraction.

The **Heimathues** collects and maintains cultural history. The typical Black Forest house is over 250 years old.

The old mine in the district **Mättle** has been accessible for visitors as **presentation mine** since 2000. It was officially mentioned for the first time in 1798. Iron pyrites were mined until the closure of the **Vitriolhütte** in the district **Berghütte** in 1835.

Local exhibitions are held in the Heimathues of Todtmoos.

The house where Hans Thoma was born in Bernau

Sulzburg

Sulzburg

The former **little silver mining town** of **Sulzburg** (2,700 inh.), mentioned for the first time in 821, has a historic town centre with a town hall (1834). The former Protestant town church accommodates the state **mining museum**. There is a five km long **round path** in **Sulzbach Valley** providing information on the **history of mining**. The **Romanesque church St. Cyriak**, parts of which date from the 11th c., is regarded as one of the **oldest places of worship** in southern Germany. The restored **synagogue** (1823) and **Jewish cemetery** (1550) are also worth seeing.

Müllheim, an important wine-growing locality

Bernau

Bernau (2,000 inh.) became well-known through the popular **Black Forest painter Hans Thoma** (1839-1924), a farmer's son from the district **Oberlehen**. The **Hans Thoma museum** in the **town hall** of **Innerlehen** shows many original pictures. There are two altar paintings by the artist in the church next door. The **Resenhof** (1789) has a **farm museum**. There is a beautiful hiking route leading from **Bernau village** on the **Hans-Thoma-Weg** via **Krunkelbachhütte** to **Herzogenhorn**.

Markgräflerland

The name **Markgräflerland** comes from the rule of the **margraves of Baden**, who had their seat in **Burg Baden** in **Badenweiler**. The most famous Markgräfler is the **writer Johann Peter Hebel** (1760-1826), who wrote many poems in **Alemannian dialect**. A **literary prize** named after him is awarded in his home locality **Hausen** in Wiesental. Markgräflerland has a very mild climate. The typical **wine** of the region is the **Gutedel**. The grape was brought by the Baden Grand Duke Margave Karl Friedrich von Baden from the Swiss **Vevey** to Markgräflerland around 1780.

Müllheim

Müllheim (18,000 inh.) is the **centre** of Markgräflerland. With 480 ha of vineyards, the town is the region's **largest viticulture community**. The **Müllheim wine market**, held since 1872, is regarded as the oldest Baden wine market. The **Romans** also left traces in Müllheim. Remains of a classical heating plant can be viewed in the former **parish church St. Martin**. The **Markgräfler museum** is in the **inn Krone** (1780) on the market square.

There is a magnificent view above the castle ruins (11th. c) of Baden-weiler.

Badenweiler

The **oldest spa** in Markgräflerland is **Badenweiler (3,900 inh.)**, at the foot of the **Blauen**. Here the ancient Romans already combined cleanliness and hygiene with a luxurious lifestyle.

The well-preserved old **thermal facilities** – the most recent excavations have even exposed a unique **"podium temple"** – show that a real bathing and cultural centre existed here **2,000 years ago**. The **Roman ruin**, which is protected by a roof, is one of the best preserved **bathing buildings of antiquity** in Germany. Badenweiler was officially mentioned for the first time as **"Baden"** in 1028. About a hundred years later, the **castle** was built on a rise. It had various masters over the centuries. What remained is a striking **ruin** that today overlooks the modern **spa centre**, built in the 1970s, and the spacious spa area.

A real sea of blossom – the spa centre terrace at the foot of the castle ruins in spring.

Badenweiler's rise to become a **world spa** began in the 19th c. It was visited first by the Grand Ducal pair of Baden and then the **European high aristocracy**. There is a memorial stone in the spa gardens and an exhibition in the spa centre recalling the Russian dramatist **Anton P. Chekov** (1860-1904), who died of tuberculosis while taking a health cure in Badenweiler.

The spa Badenweiler is located in a picturesque setting between vineyards and forest and has a very mild climate. The 12 ha **spa gardens** with its luxurious vegetation recall the south. It also has exotic trees such as **ginkgos** and **redwoods**. The locality is closed for **through traffic** between April and October to protect the spa area.

Badenweiler aims to preserve its nostalgic flair without losing touch with the modern age. The **Cassiopeia thermal baths** with the **marble bath** (1875) was carefully renovated and modernized in the 1990s.

Even the Romans took advantage of the curative properties of the thermal springs, as demonstrated by the remains of the Roman thermal baths.

Cassiopeia thermal baths, redesigned according to the latest balneotherapeutic principles

The bath now offers over 1,000 m² of water area. The **bathing area** is fed with **thermal water**, which bubbles at a temperature of **26.4°** from the **spring**.

Opposite the thermal baths, there is a small **cabinet** with **wax figures** by **Josefine Tussaud**. The **Grand Ducal Palace**, built in 1586 and renewed in neo-Renaissance style in 1888, is in the palace park. The old choir of the **Protestant church** is decorated with murals from the 14th c.

St. Paulskirche

Anton Tschechow

Roman stele

Schlossplatz

125

The Blauen, an impressive sight south-east of Badenweiler

Blauen

With its height of **1,165 metres** and location on the southern edge of the high Black Forest, **Blauen**, also called **Hochblauen**, is an excellent **lookout point** to the south. From the **local hill** of the spa **Badenweiler**, you can see as far as Basel with the loop of the Rhine and on clear days, particularly in autumn, the Berner Oberland. The Eiger, Mönch and Jungfrau peaks then seem to be within easy reach.

On the top of the wooded mountain there is a **TV tower** and a smaller **look-out tower**, 16 metres high. The Blauen is also a popular **starting place** for **hang-gliders**, which take to the air behind the **Berghaus Hochblauen** on the southern side. The **Altvogelbachfelsen** is located at a height of about **800 metres** on the northern slope of the Blauen above Badenweiler. It is challenge for **climbers**, but well secured with pitons.

Berghaus Hochblauen at a height of 1,165 metres

Attractive **hiking paths** lead up to the Blauen, which can also be reached by car via two routes: from the Rhine plain over Badenweiler or from the other side via Marzell.

The **Nonnenmattweiher** near **Neuenweg** is an interesting excursion destination in the hiking area between **Blauen** and **Belchen**. This small cirque was created in the last Ice Age. The **nature reserve** around the **pond** has rare flora, including Alpine plants and many types of high moor vegetation on a **peat island** floating in the middle of the lake. The lake is not far from the **long-distance foot-path Westweg** leading from Pforzheim to Basel.

On the Blauen: with good visibility, you can look over the hills of the Southern Black Forest as far as the Swiss Alps.

Kandern

Schneiderhof, which attracts visitors as museum

Kandern (8,000 inh.), founded in the 8th c., displays the masterpieces of the local **potters' guild** in the **local history and culture and ceramics museum**, a late Gothic stepped gable house. **Bürgeln Palace** (18th c.), not far from Kandern, is worth seeing. In summer, the historic **Kandertal railway** operates between Kandern and Haltingen.

The lordly rococo Bürgeln Palace

Bad Bellingen

Bad Bellingen (3,800 inh.) was a simple farming and fishing village up to 1956. Its swift rise as spa began when a thermal with water containing sodium, calcium and chloride was discovered during trial drillings for crude oil.

Balinea thermal baths, offering bathing fun on 1,000 m2 of water area

Two more springs were developed in 1972 and 1974. The modern **spa facilities** include the **Balinea thermal baths**, opened in 2000. The **spa area** with its spacious, well-kept park is located below the old centre of the locality in the **Rhine plain**. Pedestrians can also overcome the height difference with a **lift**.

The **town hall** is an interesting building in the centre of the town, which has retained its village character. The late Gothic main building, built in 1590 as **palace** of the counts of Andlau, is connected with a modern **tower with steps**. The **parish church** situated higher up has a choir from the 17th c. The history of medicinal baths from the Romans to the present day is told by the **Upper Rhine baths and local history and culture museum** in the district **Bamlach**.

Spa centre

Regional politics are discussed in the Bad Bellingen town hall with its striking stepped gable.

Schliengen

Schliengen (5,100 inh.) in Markgräflerland is set among vines and fruit trees. It is known for its wine and its kirschwasser. The **wine instruction path** and **winepressmuseum** with a winepress from the 17th c. are informative. The **moated castle Entenstein** (1525) is today seat of the community administration. There was probably a residential tower around 1000 at this place. Another sight is the **parish church St. Leodegar** with its rococo pulpit and beautiful side altars.

Weil am Rhein

Sights of the border town **Weil am Rhein (29,500 inh.)** are the modern **Vitra architectural park** and **Vitra design museum**. The Laguna Badeland with swimming pool with wave movement and **giant water chute** are magnets for visitors. The **Dreiländergarten** (garden of three states) formed the centre of the state horticultural show in 1999.

Parish church St. Leodegar in Schliengen

Weil am Rhein museum of local history and culture

Basel

An excursion to the neighbouring Basel is a "must".

Basel (187,000 inh.) is the centre of **north-west Switzerland**, on the border between **Germany and France**. The German-speaking cultural, educational and economic centre is a **historic town** with old traditions, such as the well-known **Basel carnival**. Features of the **old town** are the **minster** donated in **1019** by Heinrich II, 16th c. town hall and **Spalentor** (1370).

The founding of Basel goes back to the **1st c. BC.** Highlights of its history include the **Council** (1431-48). The **university** was opened in 1460, and in 1501 Basel joined the **Swiss Confederation**. Basel is a city with many green areas and parks. Its zoo is very popular.

The town hall of Basel with its striking high tower

The very cheerful-looking medieval Spalentor with its colourful tiles.

Lörrach

The county town **Lörrach (47,000 inh.)** at the exit of the Wiesen Valley is the economic and cultural centre of **Upper Baden**. It was mentioned for the first time in the 11th c. and has had a **town charter** since 1682. Its industrial development began in the mid-18th c. with the establishment of the first **textile factory**. The Lörrach townscape is modern with the **Zundelheim fountain** as symbol and the high-rise building with the town administration. The **prehistoric findings**, sculptures and painting in the **museum at the Burghof** are worth seeing.

Rötteln Castle, the largest in Upper Baden

Old market square of Lörrach

Rötteln Castle in the district **Hagen** has had an eventful history. The **fortress** built in the 13th c. was one of the largest castles in the region in the Middle Ages. It was burnt down in 1678. Even as ruin, it still looks impressive with its massive walls and towers. It is a **venue for open-air events** in summer.

Rheinfelden

Rheinfelden (32,500 inh.) was created after the completion of the Baden **High Rhine rail line Basel-Säckingen** in 1856 opposite the **Swiss town of the same name** on the Rhine. Its industrial upturn began with the **run-of-river power station,** built in 1898, the first of its type on the **High Rhine**. Further run-of-river power stations were built in the neighbouring communities **Grenzach-Wyhlen** in 1912 and near **Schwörstadt** in 1932. Rheinfelden is the final station for Rhine shipping. In **Dinkelberg** near **Beuggen** located upriver, there are two **caves**: **Tschamberhöhle** with a grotto with spring and underground waterfalls and **Nagelfluhhöhle**. The caves are open only in summer.

Oberrheinplatz, Rheinfelden

The longest wood-covered bridge in Europe is in Bad Säckingen.

Bad Säckingen

A real **love story** made **Bad Säckingen (16,600 inh.)** famous. The marriage between the aristocratic Maria Ursula von Schönau and the ordinary castle trumpeter Werner Kirchhofer in 1657 gave the writer **Johann Victor von Scheffel** (1826-86) the material for his romantic epic **"Der Trompeter von Säckingen"** ("The Trumpeter of Säckingen"), published in 1853. Scheffel was made an **honorary citizen** of the town and elevated to the nobility.

Schönau Palace, also known as **"Trompeterschlösschen"**, has a comprehensive collection of trumpets.

Waldshut was created on a former **Rhine island**. The Irish **monk Fridolin** founded a settlement here in the 6th c. The Fridolinstag with procession is celebrated in his honour in March. A convent called **"Seckinga"**, mentioned for the first time in **878**, determined the fate of the region for centuries. The Fridolinsmünster (13th c.) with its **precious relics** is evidence of the rich past. The old **Gothic church** was converted in baroque style in the 18th c.

The minster is adjoined by Palais Landenberg, used as town hall since

The wooden bridge (1571) spans the Rhine to the Swiss side.

The twin towers of the Fridolinsmünster, visible from afar

The interior of the baroque church with its exquisite ecclesiastic treasures and murals

1850. Behind the minster, Kater Hiddigeigei, known from the "Trompeter von Säckingen", is immortalized. The tomb of the legendary trumpeter is on Münsterplatz. The magnificently painted house Zur Fuchshöhle is a sight on the north-west side of the market square.

An attraction of Waldhut is the **longest wood-covered bridge in Europe** with a length of 200 metres. The first Rhine bridge to the Swiss bank was already mentioned in the 13th c. The people of Säckingen had to build a new bridge several times after it had been burnt down or destroyed by flooding. Historic buildings in the vicinity of the Rhine bridge are the house of the Teutonic Order, the rococo house and the Scheffelhaus.

The **spa area with its mineral baths and clinics** is located above the town. The **Bad Säckingen thermal springs** were already very popular in the Middle Ages. Two passenger ships offer excursions on the Rhine in the summer half of the year.

Schönau Palace (16th-17th c.)

Trumpeter at Schönau Palace

Bacon and schnapps

The traditional **Black Forest snack** consists of a nice piece of **gammon** smoked with fir branches, hearty **bread** baked in a wood stove and a tot of **schnapps**. The more lavish version includes **black pudding and liver sausage** and a smoked **farmer's style sausage**. The schnapps doesn't have to be a **Black Forest kirschwasser**: it can also be another type of spirits distilled from fruit – Obstler, Rossler or Tobinambur, Zwetschenwasser, Williams Christ or Himbeergeist. There is a wide variety of aromatic **"Wässerle"** and **"Geister"** from **Black Forest distilleries**.

The fruit for the original Black Forest kirschwasser ripen in the foothills of the Rhine plain and in the valleys. In **spring**, the **cherry-growing areas** are transformed into an enchanting white **sea of blossoms**. The **"Brennkirschen"**, the cherries for distilling, which are smaller and sweeter than the **"Tafelkirschen"** (table cherries), are harvested at the beginning of summer and filled in mash barrels or tanks. With the fermentation, the sugar in the fruit turns into alcohol. The subsequent **distilling** of the **mash** calls for great skill from the schnapps distillers. The high-proof alcohol running out of the **boiler** is then diluted to drinking strength – generally between **45 and 50 percent** – and stored for a while (connoisseurs swear by a period of at least **two years**). All schnapps made from **stone** and **pomaceous** fruits are distilled with this procedure. **Berries** are **steeped** in alcohol before distilling, as their natural fruit sugar content is insufficient for fermentation. In quite a few areas, Rossler or **Topinambur** is produced from the sweet-tasting **tuber** of a **type of sunflower** that was imported from **North America** in the 17th c. Because it is also suitable as fodder, the plant is also called **"horse potato"**.

Hearty Black Forest fare

Black Forest houses

Fürstenberger Hof in Zell-Unterharmersbach

The most striking characteristic of the Black Forest house is its **pulled-down roof**. As **"all-in-one house"**, it accommodates people, animals and harvested crops under one roof. The typical **Black Forest thatched roof** – covered with straw skilfully laid in strengths of 50 centimetres offering natural protection against the elements for over a hundred years – is not a common sight nowadays. The most impressive thatched roof homesteads are meanwhile museums, such as **Vogtsbauernhof** in the open-air museum of the same name in **Gutach** and **Fürstenberger Hof** in **Zell-Unterharmersbach**. In the High Black Forest, the homesteads are covered with wooden shingles.

Romantic typical Black Forest houses with roofs covered with shingles or straw

Wehr

The most famous native of **Wehr (13,100 inh.)** is the **world-famous** violin soloist **Anne-Sophie Mutter**,

Looking towards Wehra

St. Martin in Wehr

who grew up in the little town and at the tender age of 25 became an **honorary citizen** of the town in 1988. There is a modern bronze sculpture of the artist at **Storchenplatz**.

Fountain in the main street of Schopfheim

Wehr was officially mentioned for the first time in 1092. Traces in the **old townscape** have been left by the lords of Schönau, who ruled in **Wehratal** between 1365 and 1853. Around 1570 they built the **Old Palace**, which was followed in 1748 by the **New Palace**, an imposing baroque building. From the mid-19th c., Wehr developed into a centre of industry of the Upper Rhine. An interesting place to visit is the **Erdmann stalactite cave**, a unique natural monument, near **Hasel**.

Schopfheim

The **Romans** settled in **Schopfheim (19,500 inh.)** before it was mentioned for the first time in **807**. Konrad von Rötteln raised the locality to the status of town in 1250. The **church St. Michael** (1482) with its high tower, once part of the **town fortifications**, is worth seeing. A **natural phenomenon** is **Eichener See**, which rises and falls with the water level in the **karst** of **Dinkelberg**. The **bird park** in the neighbouring **Steinen** with over 300 species is a popular attraction for families. Destinations with good views for hikers are **Hoher Flum**, at a height of 535 metres near **Schopfheim**, and **Zeller Blauen** (1,077 metres) near **Zell in Wiesental**.

Laufenburg

The **Baden Laufenburg (8,400 inh.)** and **Swiss Laufenburg** were once one town. The **Rhine** has formed the border since the Peace of Luneville in 1801. The two towns are linked by a **bridge over the Rhine**, which was already mentioned in 1207. The **medieval past** is well preserved in both Laufenburgs with their picturesque little lanes, fountains, towers and gates. Above Laufenburg is the village of **Hochsal**, known for its **church tower**, which is regarded as the symbol of **Hotzenwald**.

High Rhine

The **High Rhine** is the name of the **145 km** long stretch of the **Rhine** between **Lake Constance** and **Basel**. It marks the **southern edge** of the Black Forest. The **river** flows through a delightful landscape between **Hotzenwald** and the **Swiss Jura**, forming with a few exceptions the border between **Germany** and **Switzerland**.

After the **High Rhine** has left **Lake Constance** at the Untersee, it flows initially as a broad, quiet river. However, on the way to Basel it is soon confronted by the hard **Jura limestone**, which narrows the river-bed or forms sills in the river. At the famous **Schaffhausen Rhine falls**, the Rhine plunges down over a limestone ledge **23 metres** high. The course of the river is continually defined by the Jura limestone up to Basel. At the **Rhine bend of Eglisau**, the river meets the hard rock again and is diverted in a north-westerly direction to the Upper Rhine Plain.

It's a delightful experience enjoying the landscape on the High Rhine from an **excursion boat**. Passenger ships are deployed between Laufenburg and Schwörstadt. **Bad Säckingen** also has a ship landing stage. From **Waldshut** there are excursion trips as well as a ferry link to **Full** in **Switzerland**.

A trip with **High Rhine railway** is also an impressive and very interesting experience. The route leads from the **Baden station** in **Basel** via Bad Säckingen and Waldshut-Tiengen to the Swiss **Schaffhausen.**

Morning mist on the Rhine

Albsee near St. Blasien

Ice Age lakes

The Black Forest mountains bore thick **ice caps two to three million years ago**. The ice masses expanded the valleys, causing the slopes to rise and creating deep inclines. The last Ice Age ended about **10,000 years** ago, but its traces are still to be seen today, the most beautiful legacy being the **Ice Age lakes.**

Cirque lakes such as **Feldsee** at the foot of the Feldberg and **Nonnenmattweiher** in the Belchen area were created in hollows. The **Titisee**, the **largest natural lake** in the Black Forest, dammed up at the end moraine of a glacier tongue from the Feldberg.

The **nine cirque lakes** in the North-

ern Black Forest typically have a round shape and dark water. The most well-known is **Mummelsee** on the **Black Forest mountain road**. There used to be 60 lakes, but most have been filled up by sedimentation.

The Black Forest **high moors** were also created after the Ice Age. The **largest** still intact high moor with beautiful moor lakes is the **nature reserve** around **Wildsee** and **Hohloh-See**, near **Kaltenbronn** in the vicinity of **Bad Wildbad**. The floating **peat island** in **Buhlbach-see** near Baiersbronn-Obertal is also an ecological rarity.

Twin town Waldshut-Tiengen

The twin town **Waldshut-Tiengen (22,500 inh.)** is regarded as gateway to the **Black Forest** and bridge to Switzerland. Old finds prove that **Waldshut** was originally a **royal palatinate** of the **Carolingians**.

The **palatinate above the Rhine bank** became a town under the Zähringer. It is said to have been founded in 1249. Under King Rudolf von Habsburg, the town assumed its extent that is still recognizable today in the **old town**.

The people of Waldshut have never forgotten the **summer of 1468**. The fortunate end of the siege by the Swiss is celebrated every year in the large **Waldshut local festival**, the **Chilbi**.

The centre of Waldshut is formed by **Kaiserstrasse**, a long street market stretching between the **upper** and l**ower town gate**. The middle-class houses from the 16th-18th c. clearly show the influence of the neighbouring **Switzerland**.

Historic Chibli Festival

A Rhine ferry plying between the banks

Kaiserstrasse, marked off by the upper and tower town gate

Tiengen

Tiengen, the gate to **Klettgau** with its idyllic **wine villages**, has an **old town** full of nooks and crannies with the striking **Storchenturm**, **palace** of the princes of Schwarzenberg and **palace church St. Maria** (1753), designed by the famous Vorarlberg architect **Peter Thumb**. The Roman settlement was officially mentioned for the first time in 868. With its large **local festival**, the **Schwyzertag**, Tiengen still celebrates its successful defence against an attack by the Duke of Urslingen in 1415.

Küssaburg

The keep of **Küssaburg Castle ruins**, located south-east of Tiengen, offers a magnificent view of the landscape. A Heinrich I, Count of Küssenberg, was spoken of for the first time in 1177. The giant castle complex on the Küssaberg, 629 metres high, set in the middle of a **nature reserve**, was destroyed in 1634, when it was burnt down by its own garrison to prevent it falling into the hands of the approaching Swedish troops under General Horn. It has been a ruin ever since.

The parish church St. Maria von Tienagen with its impressive tower

Tiengen does not only have a palace.

Küssaburg on the Küssaberg, 629 metres high

Day excursions to Lake Constance
Constance, Mainau, Birnau, Lindau, Meersburg

The old castle of Meersburg, Germany's oldest inhabited castle

The Schaffhausen Rhine Falls is among

It's only a stone's throw from the Southern Black Forest to **Lake Constance**, the **Swabian Sea**. Constance (80,000 inh.) is the largest **Lake Constance town** and a university centre. The **Council of 1414-18**, the highlight of the town history, is still evident everywhere. The plenary session of the cardinals convened in the **minster Unserer Lieben Frau**. Pope Martin V was elected in the **former department store**, today called Council, and the **Rota** held court in the old **church St. Stephan**. A modern attraction is the **Sea Life Center** with its aquariums holding 3,000 local fish.

The visitor feels as if transported to

The uniquely beautiful location of the island town of Lindau.

...argest waterfalls in Europa. Enormous masses of water thunder down in spring.

paradise on the **flower island Mainau** in Lake Constance. The **Aboretum** with 500 species of deciduous and coniferous trees forms the heart of the magnificent gardens on Mainau with its palms, citrus fruits and orchids ensuring **exotic flair**.

A jewel on the opposite Lake Constance bank is the **St. Mary's pilgrimage church Birnau**, a splendid 18th c. baroque building.

The defiant castle from the 7th c. and the **New Palace** (1750) with its baroque facade are keynotes of **Meersburg (5,500 inh.)**. The poetess **Annette von Droste-Hülshoff** (1797-1848) spent her last years in **Fürstenhäusle**.

The **Unteruhldingen lake dwelling museum** gives an idea of life in the **Stone and Bronze Age**.

The old town of **Lindau** boasts magnificent buildings with attractive facades and mighty **stepped gables**. A spectacular **natural show** is offered by the **Rhine Falls** near **Schaffhausen**, where the Rhine plunges over a 23 metre high cliff into the depths. There is a **fireworks display** on the rocks on the **Swiss national holiday**.

This dazzling spectacle is offered on the Swiss national holiday.

The flower island Mainau in Lake Constance has an impressive variety of flora and fauna.

Baroque jewel Birnau

Goodbye to the Black Forest

Dear reader, we trust that you have enjoyed visiting our beautiful Black Forest and that our guide has been helpful and will also bring back some pleasant memories. We hope you'll visit us again soon.

BLACK FOREST – important addresses

Southern Forest – important addresses
Stadtstraße 2, 79104 Freiburg
Tel: 07 61/21 87-3 04, Fax: 07 61/21 87-5 34, E-mail: tss@rrz-freiburg.de

Schwarzwald Tourismus GmbH (Central Black Forest)
Geschäftsstelle Offenburg, Gerberstraße 8, 77652 Offenburg
Tel: 07 81/9 23 77 77, Fax: 07 81/9 23 77 70
E-mail: mail@schwarzwald-tourismus.com

Tourism in the Nothern Black Forest
Postfach 100666, 75106 Pforzheim, Tel: 0 72 31/1 47 38-0
Fax: 0 72 31/1 47 38-20, E-mail: touristik@noerdlicher-schwarzwald.de

Black Forest info and brochure service
Futura Marketing GmbH, Prospekt-Service-Hotline: 0 18 05/66 12 24
Fax: 0 18 05/66 12 25, E-mail: prospektservice@schwarzwald-tourist-info.de

Black Forest info and brochure service
Schwarzwald Tourismus GmbH, Ludwigstraße 23, 79104 Freiburg

Freiburg Wirtschaft und Touristik GmbH & Co. KG
Rotteckring 14, 79098 Freiburg
Tel: 07 61/38 81-8 80, Fax: 07 61/3 70 03
E-mail: touristik@fwt-online.de, www.fwt-online.de

Baden-Baden Kur & Tourismus GmbH
Solmsstraße 1, 76530 Baden-Baden
Tel: 0 72 21/27 52 06, Fax: 0 72 21/27 52 61, E-mail: bbt@baden-baden.com

Dear reader,
SCHÖNING-VERLAG would like to thank you for having purchased our product. We know that you will enjoy it as travel guide and souvenir.
Please don't hesitate to contact us if you have any suggestions or queries. These travel guides have been published on many German towns, cities and regions and frequently translated into other languages. We are continually expanding the series.
Please also visit our website: www.schoening-shop.de